THE GOLDEN HOUR.

BY

MONCURE D. CONWAY,
AUTHOR OF "THE REJECTED STONE."

Impera parendo.

NEGRO UNIVERSITIES PRESS
NEW YORK

Originally published in 1862
by Ticknor and Fields

Reprinted from a copy in the collections
of the Brooklyn Public Library

Reprinted 1969 by
Negro Universities Press
A DIVISION OF GREENWOOD PUBLISHING CORP.
NEW YORK

SBN 8371-2683-5

PRINTED IN UNITED STATES OF AMERICA

CONTENTS.

ONCE upon a time an innkeeper, awakened at midnight by caterwaulings in the hall below, was filled with wrath, and, leaping from his bed, seized a poker, and rushed down stairs to demolish the cats. But he did not wait to light a lamp for the expedition. The unexpected results were, that, in striking at the cats, he broke the hall-clock, and the hall-lamp; then, falling, he broke his right arm, broke two teeth out, and sprained an ankle.

In fine, he hit and hurt nearly everything *except* the cats.

At such a cost the innkeeper learned that blindfold zeal can do but harm.

— Twenty millions of men and women, whose hands ply daily sword or needle, compelled by a purpose too great for them to define; a million men, marching and eagerly awaiting the order to march toward the valley of death; manifold Abrahams, standing beside their sons, whom their faith has bound and laid on altars of sacrifice; — are not these signs of a vitality and zeal in any nation adequate for any emergency?

But where is the lamp for these? How many more blunders and bruises must we have ere we demand light upon this stairway, on which we can climb, down which we may fall? Thus far in this war nearly everything has been zealously struck, EXCEPT THE REAL FOE OF THIS NATION.

The writer of these pages, having for a long time studied

this wild disease at the South, which has made that section into its own image and likeness, — having been brought by destiny face to face with this evil in the South, whose spots of contagion he has also marked on every institution of the North, — believes that this nation has but one foe, and that it will be pursued by that one everywhere and always until it is no more evaded, but met and destroyed, as it easily can be.

Convinced that the arch-traitor is not Davis, but Slavery, and that the age is worthy of an army of saviours, who shall, by its destruction, rescue, besides the Union, both slave and rebel, I send forth this work, trusting that it may help forward the day when the only war-cry of our nation shall be, — MERCY TO THE SOUTH! DEATH TO SLAVERY!

THE GOLDEN HOUR.

I.

POINT OF PERSPECTIVE.

THERE are in the United States — as we are face-
tiously termed — nearly thirty-four millions of human
beings.

Of these, three hundred and forty-eight thousand, or
about one ninety-eighth of our population, are owners
of slaves.

This small proportion has, ever since this was a nation,
preserved in our midst every old form which the nation
meant to abandon; just as if we had never had a May-
flower or Bunker Hill, the old autocracies and aristocra-
cies gathered about the rich board of the New World,
the thirty-three millions and two thirds standing behind
the chairs of the handful constituting the caste of
Owners of Human Beings. For this ninety-eighth of
their number the millions must pour out their hard
earnings to buy new territory; for this, pour out their
blood to rob Mexico of territory; for this, fear to call
their souls their own.

It made no difference that these lived in so-called

Free States. Did they go South, they must go crawling; or West, it must be to build the highways of America as convicts with Slavery's ball and chain tied to their feet; whilst at home they saw their sacred growths, Religion, Education, Literature, and Social Science, with a worm gnawing at every core.

At length this pitiful handful, having blighted a hundred thousand square miles of the finest land in the world, having kept uncultivated thrice as much more, having locked up in impenetrable barriers the richest metals on the continent, having produced an average of a hundred thousand white adults in every Southern State who cannot read or write, having kept the whole country in discord and hot water for two generations, have finally plunged it into civil war.

Of the 348,000 owners of slaves in America, only 18,000, at the highest estimate, are loyal; and these, being generally in the Border States, where large plantations of slaves are not found, own an average of 2½ slaves apiece.

One fortnight's expenses of the present war would pay $ 500 for each slave held by any person at present pretending to be loyal.

A man once saw a fiery dragon descending the side of a distant mountain: starting back in terror, his eye reached a true point of perspective, and he perceived that the dragon was the minutest of spiders, which had swung itself down too close to his eye for right vision.

II.

IN CHANCERY.

IF there were no question of the suppression of a vast rebellion involved in the present relations of the nation with Slavery, it would be a momentous question how this small slaveholding interest has gained such an ascendency in the government that it is not held as attainted even by treason. Are these slaveholders, in number about equal to the population of one of our third-rate cities, the royal family of a king that can do no wrong? It is a question of some interest to thirty millions of men, who, fondly imagining themselves living under a democratic government, see their rulers suspending universal guaranties of Liberty rather than touch the right of eighteen thousand men to do wrong, — pulling down the very rafters of the house, rather than destroy the rats' nests.

Before this nation stand two classes of subjects. The one is a class of those who, having received every benefit at the hands of the nation, and no burden, have yet betrayed and wronged it, and inflicted every stab they could upon it. The other class is of those who have received at the hands of the nation nothing but degradation and wrong, who, having every reason to betray it, have yet never betrayed it or harmed it. And, lo, between these two the nation prefers to let its severest blow fall on the poor man it has wronged, even when he would befriend it, though it strengthen the arms which threaten its life and the lives of its bravest children !

Can any one account for the infatuation which seizes our public men whenever they catch a glimpse of an African, or anything that concerns an African? How often have we got hold of some man whom we thought a free-soiler, and sent him to Washington only to see him at the first step on its threshold turn out a soiler of freedom! Æsop tells of a cat which had been transformed into the form of a woman. On one occasion, sitting at a table with a company, none of which suspected that she was really a cat, a mouse made its appearance on the floor ; whereupon, forgetting the human part she was playing, this feline female leaped forward, upset the table, and devoured the mouse before the astonished company. *Moral:* Instinct will tell, under whatever forms. Never be sure that your politician, however transformed he may seem, is a genuine man, until you have seen a negro pass safely within reach of his official paw.

Get close enough to the interior life of an American politician, and you will be pretty sure to find that it stands in his religious faith, that the stripes in our flag have a Swedenborgian correspondence to stripes on a black man's back. It is to be feared that in this they represent the prejudice or the indifference of the people. Lately I saw two negroes thrust from a

car in New York, on a night so stormy and bitter
that it would have been cruel to expel a brute. A
dog in the same car slept at the feet of his master,
undisturbed.

Thus is Slavery rotting the very heart of Manhood
throughout this country.

We have learned nothing of Slavery, if we have not
learned this truth, to wit, — THAT SLAVERY HAS NO WILL
OF ITS OWN. There has been a delusion in this country,
that Slavery is a free-agent; and when, in Kanzas,
the ballot of Freedom was responded to by the torch
and bowie-knife, — when, in the whole nation, the ballot
was replied to by a bomb into Fort Sumter, — we began
to awake to the perception that Slavery has no free
choice. Slavery is more a slave than any man it fetters.
It had no choice but to fire on Sumter. Chemistry
does not more by fixed laws make a boulder, than by
fixed laws Slavery hurls it at the head of Wendell
Phillips. Slavery is in the coils of Fate, and must,
if it exists, obey its own dark laws.

The other day a man — and that is a rarer creature
than is generally supposed — stood upon the soil of
Virginia. Slavery said, "He is firm, truthful, intelligent, — the gamest man I ever saw," — then proceeded
to hang him. Slavery would have hung him had it
been Jesus Christ, because it must.

The common sense of the country has already come
to the conclusion that Slavery is the cause of the war.
But it must be seen that war is the legitimate appen-

dage and weapon of Slavery; that Slavery is perpetual
war; that *this* war is but the effort to extend Slavery's
already existing martial law over the entire government. Only by military power has Slavery been retained in this country. In the cities of the North,
when its claim to some fugitive was to be asserted,
we have seen its martial array; but this was only the
cropping out of the constant state of things in the
South. Nightly patrols; the punishment of men from
the North without process of law; the frequent suppression of the usual laws for reasons of state; the
suppression of all discussion concerning Slavery; —
these are possible only where martial law is habitual.
The present war is only the extension and exasperation
of what has been all along the method in the war of
the strong race against the weak in the South.

It would seem, then, in the light of simple equity,
that the *natural* method of suppressing Slavery's rebellion would be found in some way of dealing with Slavery itself. ·Nature has the penalties of violating her
laws always in the direction of the transgression itself;
a fall bruises, putting one's hand in fire is followed by
a burn; and every habitual sin, as licentiousness or
drunkenness, is followed by a train of diseases pecu-
liarly its own, and growing out of its own organic character. There is no confusion of penalties; one is
not burnt by falling, nor bruised by fire.

This way we have of seizing the sword on every
occasion to punish or meet indiscriminately all attacks,

is barbarous. In the laws of this universe, where every sin has its own penalty, the retribution never fails of being effectual. The child which has once put its hand to the fire, never repeats the experiment. Nations and men must translate these great laws of Nature, and then their defences will never be of doubtful strength.

The rebellion of Slavery should at once have been followed by our only logical reply, — the abolition of Slavery.

Suppose that, in reply to that bomb which fell into Fort Sumter, our President had seized the pen, instead of the sword, and written such a proclamation as this : —

"Slavery, from being a domestic institution in certain States, with which the government had nothing to do, having become the common foe of all the States, with which the government has everything to do, it is hereby declared that all the slaves in this country are free, and they are hereby justified in whatever measures they may find necessary to maintain their freedom. Loyal masters are assured that they shall be properly compensated for losses resulting from this decree."

Every rebel owning a slave, or living within miles of one, would, as by the wand of an enchanter, have remained spell-bound at his fireside, where he ought to be. There could have been no war.

III.

IN COMMON LAW.

DURING a residence of some years at Washington, I found that there was a clause in the Constitution used there, which I have vainly looked for in my copy : it ran as follows : —

" Art. —, Sec. —. Any legislation on the part of Congress liable to the charge of being morally right shall be held as *prima facie* unconstitutional ; this, however, shall not invalidate such legislation, if it can be proved that its moral character is simply a coincidence."

I have seen good Republicans grow red in the face with showing that they were maintaining freedom simply for strategy or expediency, and indignantly avowing that they were not actuated by any motives of humanity or rectitude.

So we must not dwell upon any such little point as the moral ulceration of a whole nation, so much as upon the prospective waving of the Stars and Stripes on the custom-house in Charleston.

But, even in the eye of the organic law, we maintain that the right to abolish Slavery is antecedent to the right of taking the sword. It is the duty of the President to " suppress insurrections " ; but there is no intimation that the Executive shall, in suppressing insurrections, be confined to the method of bloodshed. If, indeed, bloodshed is the only method or the best method, he is sworn not to shrink from that ; but if the end could be reached by anything more humane, it is his duty to remember that the sword is termed the *ultima ratio*, — the *last* resort of states.

If in the present case there was a probability that the insurrection could be put down without bloodshed, say by slaveryshed, it were the legal duty of our President to try the slaveryshed first. When the alternative is the dreadful one of civil war, the method which dealt directly through Slavery the paralytic stroke would not demand, any more than a naval expedition, a certainty, but merely a probability, of success.

Amongst all the rights which have been claimed for Slavery, as guaranteed in the Constitution, there is one which no man has ever been bold enough to try and make out; that is, THE RIGHT OF EXISTENCE. Slavery has the right to the rendition of fugitives, — so long as it exists; the right of representation, — so long as it exists ; but nowhere the right to exist. Our fathers did not expect it to continue in existence, and made no arrangement to secure it should that existence be threatened.

Its right to be let alone in the States where it exists is simply a negative right, held " during life or good behavior " ; and our fathers were not such knaves as to guarantee its life, nor such fools as to guarantee its good behavior.

Leaving out of the account any demand of military

necessity that every slave's chain should be struck off by a decree of emancipation, it is important to bear in mind that our President has no oath registered to protect Slavery. The counterpart of the right of Slavery to be let alone in the States where it confines itself, is the forfeiture of any claim to protection from any influence in Nature or Civilization which may threaten its existence. If by lifting his finger the President could save Slavery from death, he would have no right to lift his little finger; it would be as unconstitutional to save it in any State, as it would be, under the usual and peaceful process of government, to destroy it in any State by an official act.

In the present conflict, Slavery has cast itself directly across the track where the President has sworn to engineer the government, and he has no right even to put down the brakes to save it from being cut in two. He has stretched his constitutional authority to the utmost in having sounded the whistle to warn it, as he did recently in his special message.

Let it be remembered that the right of the States to regulate their own domestic institutions is one growing out of the nature of the government which our Constitution established. But the friends of Slavery have of late years been pressing this feature of our government so far as to break it, — carrying it so far that the national government was represented as something which *had* a use, but, having created various sovereign States, was now only fit to be thrown away, like a pod from which the peas have been gathered. To put the case beyond the reach of prejudice, let us imagine a case which cannot occur, but which is parallel: Cotton is a staple which any State has a right to produce. But suppose some year all the cotton planted should bear a fatally poisonous flower, which should be woven into garments deadly to the wearers. Suppose that it was determined that, owing to some new atmospheric conditions, the cotton-plant if grown must continue a fatal poison. Then, if any State should persist in raising and selling that staple, the United States would be compelled to interfere to prevent it. No specific power would be necessary for such interference; for such a State would be an outlaw with which *any* nation (*a fortiori* that to which it owed allegiance) would have a right to interfere. Now, Slavery having always spread *malaria* throughout the nation, has this year actually borne a poisonous harvest, — which, uninterfered with, must prove fatal to republican government. Then the general government has a right to deal with it no longer as a domestic institution, but as a public foe. 'T is its duty, even in the Border States, where the crop comes on later, to arrest the institution before it has reached the fatal maturity of treason there also. Already we have heard Garrett Davis advise Kentucky to resist laws of the United States.

The question whether Slavery is a national or a State institution is this year a sheer impertinence. I have observed that, when Slavery wants new territory or a fugitive negro, it is always a national institution; when it wants discussion throttled, or, in the pathetic words of Jeff., " to be let alone," it is always a State institution. According to the States-Rights interpretation, our fathers put it together in the hasty way in which the marvellous dog spoken of in the advertisements of Spalding's glue was put together. The dog, being cut in two, was instantly made whole by this wonderful preparation ; but so hastily were the parts put together, that the hind-legs and fore-legs projected in opposite directions. So the dog went through the remainder of his life running on his fore-legs until he got tired, then turning a summerset and running on his hind-legs. Slavery having gone, as its advantages suggested, now on national, now on State legs, has at length thrown itself across the nation's track, and, if the train comes in " on time," will be cut in two once more ; and, though our Border-State friends are already offering in advance Spalding's genuine, dog-cheap, let us hope that *this* dog has had his day.

In all the States which have seceded, the gate of liberation has been opened by purblind oppression's own hand. If, as this government declares, Slavery is a State institution, it must, in the eyes of this government, fall when the State government falls. A number of " the weaker brethren " in Congress have raised a cry that this position concedes what the rebels claim, that a State can be wrested from the Union ; and Mr.

Montgomery Blair has given a blatant assent to that cry. I will not say that these men thus prove themselves unfit to legislate for a nation whose institutions they thus estimate; but if the following statements shall lead any mind to that inference, I shall not complain of being misunderstood.

Where is the court or power in any seceded State which this government can recognize? Suppose the Governor of any seceded State should claim from Governor Andrew of Massachusetts the return of a criminal to that State. Would the Governor, who is bound to return persons accused of crime to the *States* in which the crimes were committed, return a criminal to Governor Pickens?

Suppose even a loyal Carolinian to claim a negro within our lines at Port Royal, in what court is the case to be decided? There is no court, large or small, in that State, which could be recognized without surrendering the whole case of the United States. Even if the United States had a Commissioner there for the purpose, he cannot even try the case except the claimant bring a certificate of ownership from a loyal court in that State; but where will such a court be found?

This principle would be at once seen if it referred to white-faced minors and apprentices. If a few thousand of these should desert the South for our lines, and the parents and 'prentice-masters, loyal or rebel, should seek to have them returned, as " owing service " under the laws of their States, would our government treat such State codes as still in existence? Would this government return a few regiments of youths under age, who wished to fight for us, to their parents? Is it not anxious to draw away from rebel lines all of these it can?

It does not follow that the State, as a member of this government, has committed suicide, but only that all it has, by its own separate authority, established, is laid in ruins. The blow aimed by States' Rights at the authority of the nation strikes to the heart of those very Rights, and those alone; for the crime places the State before the supreme government in the attitude of a criminal, *whose allegiance is still perfect*, but whose rights are exactly what the supreme tribunal decides them to be.

No State can affect so much of its existence as is derived from, and dependent upon, acts of the general government. It can destroy its own courts, but not its United States District Court.

The United States is engaged in an unjustifiable war, if judged by any other theory than that the seceded States are in a state of anarchy; and anarchy is emancipation, because Slavery rests upon certain special (exclusively) State enactments, which being now withdrawn, it falls to the ground. If not, let some one show us why, of all peculiar and domestic institutions, — such as the laws punishing as criminals anti-slavery men, and also those who teach negroes to read or write, — slave-ownership alone has an ark in which to survive the deluge. If this war is a real thing with us, our government is engaged in establishing laws and their forms in places where all laws have been overthrown, with all the rights and wrongs held under them: universal law it may establish there, but not local law; and if Slavery exists any more in such localities, it will be by an act of this government, as purely arbitrary and infamous as if it imported so many slaves from Africa.

For the United States occupying Virginia to establish there the local laws and institutions which had existed in that State, any more than those of New York, is *ultra vires*. The United States not only has no such authority, but in the present case to recognize the relation of master and slave in the South is simply to follow in the fearful furrows of civil war, and sow them with the winds whose harvests shall be whirlwinds such as we are to-day reaping.

To all the technical objections offered to this position, — based on the idea of Centralization, the twin-error with State-sovereignty, — which hold that a State *cannot* violate its compact with the general government, the law replies with its maxim, *Via facti, via juris*.

But however important these views may be, the argument for Emancipation need not rest upon them: indeed, so systematically have the negroes been kept from the means of knowing their rights, that their liberty must rise upon them, clear and unmistakable, like a sunrise.

We need, then, an edict without reservation declaring that this government recognizes all men in this country as free. This edict may come from two sources : —

I. CONGRESS MAY DECLARE SLAVERY ABOLISHED.

1. By the power (Art. I. § 8) to provide for the common defence and general welfare. 2. By the duty (Art. IV. § 4) assigned the government, to guarantee to every State in this Union a republican form of government. When Congress has the manliness to see, what it requires ingenuity not to see, that the common defence is weakened and the general welfare impaired by the existence of Slavery in this country, it is under oath to abolish that system, under the first of these clauses. When it has the common sense to see that Slavery and the rebellion are united as cause and effect, and recognizes the normal hostility of Slavery towards the ballot-box, — i. e. to the republican form of government it is pledged to maintain in every State, — it is sworn no longer to harbor it in the country.

It is not to the point to say that the majority of the States which adopted the Constitution held slaves. Law is, essentially, the higher nature of man enthroned over his lower. Criminals are every day punished by laws which they pay to sustain, and acknowledge to be just and authentic. Many slaveholders voted for the principle that "all men are created equal." This question is to be considered apart from the practice of the States and individuals who made our Constitution, as much as apart from their religious persuasions.

The compromise which our fathers made with Slavery was not the one-sided affair which some new schools would have us believe. They gave protection to the system as long as it should last; but, on the other part, they gained the POWER OVER IT which such protection implies. The abolition of Slavery by Congress requires no amendment of the Constitution, simply because there is no word in the compact securing that institution from the natural effect of legislation for the general welfare. Consequently, its extinction is committed to the growth of opinion, and may be reached at any moment when the judgment of Congress shall enact that henceforth the clauses relating to " persons held to service " shall be held as applicable only to minors and apprentices.

The fact that these clauses, when adopted, were meant to protect Slavery, along with the liability of minors and apprentices, is balanced by the fact that its specific mention was left out for the very purpose of rendering its tenure insecure.

But the strictest constructionist, or the most sensitive traditionalist, will admit at once that the Slavery-institution to which our fathers gave a quasi-protection in the Constitution is quite a different thing from the Slavery-institution which it is now proposed to abolish. Slavery establishing the ballot-box over its own head is a different thing from Slavery trampling on the ballot-box. Slavery helping to rear a republican government is a different institution from that which comes with murderous weapon to strike it out of existence.

The truth is, it is a doomed institution. Our fathers pronounced sentence on it, giving it the benefit of clergy, whereof it has availed itself to the last stretch of grace. The day and deed of execution they assigned to their posterity. From us it may get a reprieve; but a pardon, never!

II. THE PRESIDENT OF THE UNITED STATES, AS COM-MANDER-IN-CHIEF OF OUR ARMY AND NAVY, MAY ABOL-ISH SLAVERY UNDER MARTIAL LAW.

This is a purely military power, and consequently Congress cannot, *under the war power*, abolish Slavery. Congress may, however, impeach the President, if, to the detriment of the Republic, he should refuse to do this.

The war power being legitimated by the Constitution, its edicts are constitutional law until repealed by due process of legislation, remaining in force after the exigency which evoked them is past. The slaves of rebels in the department lately under J. C. Fremont are legally, as under martial law he declared them, *free men;* and should any one of them sue for liberty, he could only be surrendered to his master by a decision that the President's modification of Mr. Fremont's Proclamation was *a military order of re-en-slavement, superseding ordinary process of law.*

They are either free men, or the President has, for military reasons, sent them to the dungeon of Slavery, as he has sent political prisoners to Fort Warren.

It is an error to suppose that, if the slaves were declared free by the Commander-in-Chief, the effect of such proclamation would pass away when the rebellion was suppressed. The President might, during the war, and under the power which had emancipated them, re-enslave them, — holding himself ready, in both cases, to show the military reasons for his action. He is supposed to act by necessity. But except by such military necessity and power, he could not revoke his proclamation. It would be law until unmade by Congress.

Equally is it an error to suppose that any State would be able, after the liberation of slaves by the United States, to re-enslave them.

Whilst the government recognizes as slaves those who are so by birth and by fact, yet for a State to enslave a man whom even its own laws have pronounced free, would be contrary to the article of the Constitution which secures every " person " from being arbitrarily deprived of life, liberty, or property; but that slaves liberated by the laws of the United States could not be made slaves by any State, is manifest from Art. VI. of the Constitution, which declares: " This Constitution, and the laws of the United States which shall be made in pursuance thereof, and all treaties made, or which shall be made, under the authority of the United States, shall be the supreme law of the land; and the judges in every State shall be bound thereby, anything in the Constitution or laws of any State to the contrary notwithstanding."

IV.

MILITARY NECESSITY.

It is claimed that the military general is the judge of what military necessity requires.

The military general is the judge of the methods by which certain movements are to be accomplished. It is manifest, however, that specific movements and methods are, to a great extent, determined by the great object to be accomplished by the entire system of movements. General McClellan is the judge of how to reach Richmond ; but of the object we have in reaching Richmond he is not at all the judge. The nation must assign the aim, and then its officers must decide what means are necessary to that aim. It is clear, that, if the demand of the nation were simply that our flag should wave over some forts and custom-houses from which it has been taken down, the military necessities involved would be very different from what they would be if the demand were that this rebellion should be crushed in such a way as that it should be absolutely impossible ever to have another.

The war power is not limited to a specific military movement, but extends to any aim which the people may hold as essential to the stability, peace, and honor of their country.

The war power — the power unsealed by military

necessity — is not dependent in its action upon the absolute indispensableness of the measures it proposes. It is justified in that it secures any advantage greater than the price paid. If a conflagration were sweeping through a city, and there were a probability that the blowing up of John Doe's house would arrest it, John Doe's lawful "castle" would be blown up. J. D. might give good reasons to show that the flames would presently be arrested without that measure ; but if it were probable that two houses might be saved by destroying this one, it would be done. In such emergencies the scale of values rules. The cow-shed must be sacrificed for the cabin, the cabin for the mansion, the mansion for two mansions.

Thus no advantage could be so small but it would, by martial law, justify the destruction of Slavery. If by abolishing the unmitigated curse of this land the life of one soldier could be saved, we should be the murderers of that soldier if we did not abolish it. If by slaying this pursuing demon we could bring peace to the country ten minutes sooner than without it, we should be traitors to civilization if we did not do it. For the one soldier's life, the ten minutes' additional peace, would be worth something ; the infernal thing we should pay for these must be reckoned worth less than nothing.

IN WAR SLAVERY IS THE STRENGTH OF THE SOUTH. — The institution of Slavery, which in time of peace is a weakness of the South, is in time of war, and untouched by us, strong enough to equal the numbers and means of the North. It has not yet been sufficiently considered that war and Slavery naturally consort ; war was the cradle of Slavery ; the first slaves were war-captives. In essence Slavery is the imposition of one will on another by physical force ; in that alone it differs from spontaneous or free labor. And 'war is but the acute form of the same disease. Slavery has been a perpetual training for the camp.

Every man who leaves the North for the field of battle is a laborer, and leaves so much derangement in the usual social integrity ; some wheel of the machine stops when he goes, and some deprivation ensues; but in the South the war is the vent of idlers, giving aim to lives hitherto aimless. This military life is a step in advance for the South, which has already displayed energies of which it had not been suspected. The South will not get sick of war so soon as the North, it being quite atwin with its Slavery for the South to become formally a military country. Whilst the training of Freedom has led the North every day farther from war, every day of Slavery has accustomed the South to it. The North has to go back a hundred years to reach the plane of war ; the land of Slavery never was beyond it.

In war all you have added to the world in a century is not only out of place, but in your way ; only the coarsest and rudest things avail here, and those who are most at home in the coarsest and rudest forces will, in a conflict of mere brute force, be apt to win. Now here are four millions of slaves working for the South. There being for military purposes corn and pork wanted, and not arts and elegances, all the superiority of intelligent over unintelligent labor ceases. The man who can dig a row of corn or feed swine is equal to the finest mechanic. And since every man who produces a soldier's ration points the soldier at us, just as the soldier points his gun at us, these four millions of negroes must be counted as our foes, whatever their feeling toward us.

The South is, then, at the start, twelve millions to our eighteen. But of our eighteen the women do not work in the field, and the children go to school, whereas the black women and minors do work in the field, — which, for military force, would make them nearly fifteen millions. Then we must estimate production in its relation to consumption : the black laborer, being fed at less than a third the cost of the corresponding Northern laborer, sustains at least two more soldiers in the field than the Northerner. Thus does the reign of barbarism reverse all the advantages of free over slave labor. In a conflict of mere brute force, Slavery has only to emphasize the old menace, fetter and bowie-knife, to which it is accustomed.

The North has imagined that it could bring the balance to its side by its superior wealth ; but it must be remembered, that those who get without paying for it what others have to pay for, are as rich as if they had the wherewithal to pay. Who would wish to be troubled with money, if he could get things for a dollar a year spent in cowhides ?

In the above estimate, which would make the contending parties in this country substantially equal in numerical force, it has not been forgotten that it is urged that a large portion of the Southern people are Unionists. Although the evidences of this seem to me slight, it would be, if true, of less bearing upon the question than might be at first supposed. For, no matter what a man's sympathies may be, he cannot labor in any section but he adds to the wealth of that section, and to its military stores and strength.

V.

THE TWO EDGES OF THE SWORD.

THE sword has two edges; one is turned toward the user, and never fails to give him a wound for each inflicted on his antagonist.

What does the settlement of this conquest by mere military force imply to the Free States ? They say that our army is not thorough in its *morale ;* which means, that the young man who was graduated last year is yet too full of culture and civilization to butcher his fellow-beings after the most approved Texan style. He has not forgotten that his mother and his pastor taught him to overcome evil with good. The gentleman is still, to a melancholy extent, predominant in him, the horse and alligator sadly deficient.

This moralization of the soldier is the demoralization of the man. War is the apotheosis of brutality. Looking into the past, we see it as a climax of horrors when a harlot is borne through the streets of Paris, proclaimed the Goddess of Reason ; but to-day, should the war end, the masses would seize the man whose hand reeked most with human blood, and bear him on their shoulders to the White House.

Should we continue this war long enough, we shall become the Vandals and Hessians the South says we are.

Every great achievement of civilization is in the way of war, and must be abridged. König of Germany has given it as his opinion, that distinguished generalship is inconsistent with the existence of the telegraph: in our war, both sides are cutting down all telegraph-lines which they cannot hold under military censorship.

The freedom of the press has been proved impossible in time of war.

The trial by jury — the coat of mail which Character has worn for ages — is torn away.

The Habeas-Corpus writ — " the high-water mark of English liberty " — is of arbitrary application.

A short time ago we were all uttering our horror of the prize-ring, with its brutalities. Now George

Wilkes announces that our frowning down the P. R. has crippled our military energies as a nation, and that it must be restored. Logic seconds his motion.

Here is Christianity itself, the civilization of religion: for its more genial teaching the world gave up the gods of battles, Jah and Jove with their thunderbolts, Mars with his spear, Odin with his sword. But War bids it recede: "You have heard that it hath been said, 'Thou shalt love thine enemy,' but I, War, say unto thee, ' *Kill* thine enemy.' "

Thus one by one these crown-jewels of our Humanity must be dimmed or exchanged for paste.

War stands before us to-day a fatal despot, knowing no law but the passion of the moment, prostrating the Century before the Hour ; takes the pen and plough from our hand, and gives us a sword ; melts types into bullets ; takes away the Golden Rule, and re-establishes the law of an eye for an eye and a tooth for a tooth.

With a new, wild joy all true hearts in this land were thrilled when the millions of the North rose up and declared to Slavery, Here shall thy waves be stayed ! There were many reasons for such joy : first, that there was a North, when we feared there was none ; next, that the disease of the country, which we had feared was chronic, had assumed an acute form, which is always more hopeful. We were glad, because we knew that this war was really the most pacific state of things which this country had ever known. We knew also that a single day of Slavery and its rule in this country witnessed more wrong, violence, corruption, more actual war, than all that civil war even could bring; (which conviction in my own mind, as one having lived all my life in the midst of or near that institution, I here declare unshaken by any disasters we have encountered.)

A gorilla is an admirable animal, looked at prospectively from the crocodile point of view; and so when a nation which had for years been crawling in the mud before an insolent usurper leaped to its feet, and forgot in a great moment the wretched prey for which it had crawled, it was an hour for pæans only. Every principle had been paid down for outward unity, — a unity preserving both hands, both feet, only to enter with both into hell-fire; but now a line was graven on the earth, and the nation declared it would perish rather than compromise again. The first grand step was to have the nation committed to an uncompromising attitude toward this rebellion; to make the determination to overcome it, at whatever physical cost, irrevocable.

So much gained, the best method of overcoming the rebellion would be arrived at by further reflection and discussion. The war, in its proper time and place, was noble, because spontaneous and heroic; but in this age and land it could only be an embryonic phase, to pass away before higher phases, which under its quick heats would speedily be developed.

Every higher being must, ere it is born from the

egg, pass through preceding forms. Every crab must be a trilobite and a lobster before it is born a crab. Man himself must first resemble the lower beings. As these inferior shapes have pioneered the way for the higher in the earth, so do they now in each individual case. As pioneers they are essential; but if the higher being forthcoming shall retain any of these inferior embryonic conditions, he is deformed; as when a man has a hare's lip or ape's hand. But every deformity was right in its place; every lip is at one period a hare-lip; it is a deformity only when retained where a healthy development would have gone beyond it. The birth of a nation is not different. We have struggled by some phases which allied us to lower governments: we must struggle by the war phase. The war is but the gorilla phase in our national embryo; we must see that it does not linger longer than is needed to add its contribution to the national manhood. If, when the period of purely human power arrives, the sword remains, it were as if claw and fang remained when the period of tooth and hand arrived.

Already there are unmistakable indications that the mere *military* enthusiasm in this contest is cooling, whilst the anxiety concerning the issue is deeper each day than the day before. Many of our soldiers who rushed to Washington had to be kept there by (what must be regarded) a forced decision of a United States judge; it was easily seen that, if one man could claim

the limit of enlistment, Washington would be left un-
defended. There is no longer any activity in recruiting-
stations; and, in the West, recruiting itinerants are
getting up revival meetings for the war. The appeals
of these officers to the crowd resemble those of revi-
valists imploring the unconverted to be saved. In the
same tones they beseech the youth to " close in with
the overtures," to enlist before it shall be " awfully
too late." The crowd usually remains still, as the de-
praved too often do in the revival meetings. It is certain that one or two more " Shilohs " will bring a draft
upon these profoundly impenitent young men.

In one of these meetings, in Central Ohio, I remember a tremendous sensation which was produced by an
old man, who arose and said that he had three sons,
brave as anybody's sons, and he was willing to sacrifice
them for his country; but he desired to be perfectly
sure that they were not to be sacrificed to human slavery, or to preserve it in the land ; he would not sacrifice their nail-pairings for that, or for the Union
with that.

VI.

FIGHTING THE DEVIL WITH FIRE.

THERE is nothing that the Devil so likes as that his antagonists should fight him with fire: the rascal knows that none can be so much at home where fire is concerned as he.

The wise Book says, " Be not overcome of evil, but overcome evil with good." Every victory of evil over evil leaves me as much vanquished as my enemy. Every blow that gains me the victory as a brute, loses me the victory as a man. My foe may lie dead at my feet; but beside him, in the dust I have made him bite, lies my crown of Reason, shattered. I could, then, find no wiser way of treating him than this.

To begin on the lowest plane, we may well ask ourselves, what advantage it will be to us to occupy the cities, islands, and beaches of the Southern coast. The triple-headed monster of Southern fever will drive us away from there. Our government has hitherto occupied the Southern forts with Southerners, and even they only held them nominally in summer. Now our Southerners have left us. If Southerners themselves have to move away from their coasts in summer, how long is it likely that men who have gone South now for the first time can live there? The sanitary committee has shown that we have been losing soldiers simply by dis-

ease at the rate of twenty-six regiments per annum:
if we hold the points on the Southern coast now occupied by us, it will be at thrice that cost.

Are we to enact the part of Sisyphus and his stone,
— rolling the stone of conquest southward during one
half of the year, to have it roll back again during the
other half?

Again: it is demonstrable that by any merely military victory (for that would leave Slavery undestroyed)
we should be as much conquered as the rebels.

My friend, Mr. Resist-the-Devil J. Browne, a descend-
ant of one of the Pilgrims, and now a student at Cambridge, wrote me some time ago the following account
of an event in that neighborhood : —

" Lately, our little neighbor — the village of Somerville — has been subjected to a terrible ordeal. Fancy
the amazement of the villagers, on seeing a huge anaconda marching leisurely down its main street! It
had, it seems, escaped from a circus exhibiting near the
village.

" Now, it is easy to see that a big snake, crawling
through a small village, is scarcely conducive to the re-
pose of mind of those resident therein. It is certain
that the quiet of Somerville was disturbed ; indeed,
the only quiet was in the streets, which were speedily
deserted, whilst in the houses the liveliest commotion
existed. Doors and windows were barricaded. The
snake had all out of doors to himself. At last the village concluded to have a meeting ; which was held out

of various up-stairs windows, the motions being made across streets. A man was appointed chairman on account of his high position in society, — he being at the attic window of a four-story house, — and presently a motion proceeded from the dormitory of an adjacent cottage, that the male residents who had fire-arms should take them and go forth to pursue this enemy of the commonwealth of Somerville. The motion was put to the various windows by the chairman in the attic, and carried. The men buckled on their armor, and went forth. When they got toward the outskirts of the village, they saw his royal anacondaship snoozing in a fence corner. When the monster saw them, he crawled off, and hid himself under a barn.

"The heroes returned to their homes, flushed with victory, — *Veni, vidi, vici,* in every eye ; they had pursued the foe, and he had fled before them ignominiously, the very Floyd of anacondas. 'Unbar your doors, ye noble matrons of Somerville,' they cried; 'the victory of your sons is complete.' But one timid lady asked where the anaconda was. 'Under Mr. Smith's barn,' was the reply. Then this lady inquired modestly, 'But may not a snake that is under a barn come out from under a barn ?' 'Sure enough !' 'Sure enough !' echoed from window after window ; and the lustre of victory was gone. The more it was thought of, the more it appeared that the anaconda was even more formidable concealed under the barn than in the middle of the street. The young men watched around the barn till nightfall; the snake did not budge. They repaired, heavy-hearted, to their homes. Alas! there was little rest in Somerville that night. All were sure they heard the snake trying *their* window-panes; each was sure it was lying over the roof of his or her house. The morning came on aching eyes. None wished to go out of the door, sure that the snake was waiting to drop straight down from roof or tree on their heads.

" Day succeeded day, and that snake, snugly disposed under the barn, kept the whole village vanquished. People began to desert Somerville: expiring leases in that fated village were not renewed. Somerville began to lose its reputation as a desirable place of residence. Real estate began to suffer. People went not through, but around that village: cars did not stop at its ticket-office. The students at Cambridge used to take morning walks *toward* Somerville: now, their walks were in a precisely opposite direction. In short, there was a prospect that the whole population would soon have to be taken into the Lunatic Asylum of that devoted village.

" At this juncture, a gentleman returned from a journey to his home there, and, hearing the trouble, killed a pig and placed it a rod from the barn; then he took his gun and got on top of the barn. With the ancient instinct of such devils to rush into swine, the snake soon made for the slaughtered animal. *Then this man killed the snake.*

"It is said that the circus-manager rushed up and began an argument to show that it was a constitutional anaconda ; but the man declared that his gun was also constitutionally a gun, and fired away.

"Who the man that killed the snake was, I have not yet learned : I have discovered, however, that he is not a member of the present Administration."

Does a purely military victory contemplate, or can it effect, anything beyond driving the snake under the barn ? "But," one may say, "having got it under a barn, we can keep it there." Certainly : and if that is what life is given for, — to sit beside barns, watching snakes, — then it is all right; but if any member of the National Barn Guard, or of the 500th regiment of Snake-watchers of the future, should consider "the situation" in the light of certain work he may have been in the habit of accomplishing, he may conclude that the snake is holding him, as much as he holds the snake.

When America has to swerve from the orbit of her destiny to stand guarding eight hundred thousand square miles of her territory from the ravages of rebellion ; when she has to hold her Union by military force ; when for this end our children must be turned aside from the noble aims fostered by free institutions and the arts of peace, drafted to swell and preserve the vast standing army which such a state of things would require, — then America, degraded into a military nation,

would be overcome of evil.   Her victory would fetter
most of all her own limbs.

Even trade could not stand such a condition.   The
Northwest needs the Mississippi River, but it does not
wish to sit forever, five hundred thousand strong, on
the banks of that stream, to see that it does n't flow
away again into a foreign land.   Trade can use the
river only by being able to leave it, and go home and
trade in full faith that this river will remain loyal.

It is this vanquished victory alone which the sword
can by any possibility win for us.

Has the sword ever done any but a partial and
patched work ?   In our American Revolution against
England, war was declared as justly and prosecuted as
successfully as ever before or since in the history of the
world ; but our difficulties to-day prove that the sword
did not do the work then assigned it cleanly.   The
sword had conquered victory and a forced peace ; but
then it had to hold them ; in gaining colonial independence thus it had made a giant foe, who, it knew, would
make other attempts at subjugation.   So the Colonies,
in order to combine against any possible attack from a
foreign usurper, must surrender to an internal usurper.
The Union was formed for the common defence ; it was
more a military than a civil measure.   It had to be
made *at once*.   The rights of man were compromised
for the emergency ; for all the States must combine,
whatever seeds of future disunion they might bring
with them.   We see to-day that this overswift formation

which the revolutionary method, adopted by our fathers, compelled, illustrates once more the infallible law that they who take to the sword shall perish by the sword.

VII.

LIBERTY'S LEGITIMATE WEAPON.

A PANTHER can slay seven men, if in the encounter the men have only the weapons of the panther: tooth to tooth, claw to claw, the men are inferior. But let *one* man encounter the panther, armed with his superiority to the panther, — let him bear in his hand his chemistry and art, in the fire-arm which the panther cannot invent or use, and he can slay the panther.

Slavery having challenged Liberty, Liberty has been unwise enough to select Slavery's own weapons. But with these weapons Liberty's apparent victories will be defeats ; for though the panther be driven into its den, to hold it there would be the subversion of this government, i. e. its change into a government of military force. But let her be armed with her superiority to Slavery, and she is irresistible.

The only legitimate weapon of Liberty is — LIBERTY.

It is doubtful if the nation at large will be able to see how a bold, unconditional decree of emancipation would speedily and thoroughly suppress this rebellion. God always allows some margin for human magnanimity. If this nation saw success in such a measure, it would enact it ; so would any herd of cattle. Room is allowed man for the play of motives higher than policy ; his highest success comes only when he seeks first the kingdom of justice, and then finds that all other advantages are added thereunto. " Honesty," says Whately, " is indeed the best policy ; but no honest man ever acted on that principle." Indeed, it takes an honest man to find out such policy ; those see clearly how emancipation would end the war forever, who would emancipate in any case, because it is right. Yet probabilities can be shown in the direction of our method, which are far stronger than any indicating that war can win us even a military victory over the rebellion ; probabilities more numerous and sufficient than those on which human beings act in a majority of cases.

There is a point in the South by touching which the entire military power of the South is paralyzed. Nat Turner touched that point, and, with fifty negroes behind him, held the entire State of Virginia as if stricken by catalepsy for five weeks. John Brown touched it, and, with twenty-one men, so held Virginia that, had he had a fourth of McClellan's army, he could in one month have occupied the entire State. It became a proverb, that John Brown had demonstrated the weakness of Slavery. This huge machinery of armies and numbers is a barbarism ; it is as if we built great

Roman aqueducts, ignoring the modern discovery of the water-level, which makes a hydrant in one's yard answer the same purpose, or a better. It is a rudeness far behind our civilization to think that numbers can conquer for us: numbers are as weak as they are strong. We are beyond that in our municipal governments. It is estimated that twenty policemen can conquer and disperse the largest riot or tumult that could occur in New York. Why? Because each policeman has the moral power of the nation at his back, whilst the rioters are mere bits of chaos. We do not have to set one half of a city to keep the other half in order. I have seen a half-dozen burly ruffians led to prison by a man weaker than either of them, but who had an IDEA symboled in the star on his breast, whilst the ruffians had none. When our country has an idea in this war, it need only send South a moderate police force. Nat Turner and John Brown, with stars out of heaven on their breasts, holding commissions from Almighty God to put down the organic disorder in the South, proved that Slavery cannot stir but as Freedom permits it; but McClellan, with 700,000 men under him for six months, proved that men unarmed with ideas are as unable to cope with the kindled ferocity of wrong, as they are without guns to cope with half their number of tigers. In a fearful sense our men are yet unarmed.

It is a common phrase with many of those who evi-

dently think that the Union would be nothing without
Slavery, that an edict of emancipation would not reach
or free a single slave, and, to use a favorite phrase
with certain journals, "would not be worth the paper
upon which it should be written." I observe, however, that these always end their arguments by saying,
For God's sake, do not try it! It is quite remarkable
how nervous they are, lest an edict should be put forth
which could have no effect whatever.

Have we considered well what would be the practical
bearing if our government should declare every slave
free? Slavery would by this stroke of the pen be ex-
posed to the antislavery feeling of the world. If John
Brown had a successor, he would march South under
protection of the flag under which the old captain was
hung. White and black crusaders would rise in Canada, Kansas, Ohio, Hayti, New England, following new
hermit-leaders to rescue the holy places of humanity.
Hayti would no longer need beg laborers to come to her
shores, and pay them for coming: she need only send
her ships to cruise near the inlets and creeks of the
Southern coast, and pick them up as they should
escape.

It is not to the point, observe, to say that such an
edict would not at once free the slaves practically; it
would practically do a better thing, — *it would recall to
his home, where he ought to be, every soldier now in
arms against the United States.* It is manifest that the
South would not be able to resist the antislavery cru-

sade of the world, guarding its slaves from escape, and
at the same time leave its homes to assassinate the liberties of the United States. All that a Southerner hath
will he give for his slave ; and to that cord drawing
him home would be added that panic which a whisper
of insurrection can raise in that section to such an extent that it drives all before it. In a single month
there would be a distribution of all the forces of the
Confederacy into various Home Guards.

Perhaps I am more impressed with the conviction of
the immediate potency of emancipation than persons
reared in the North. I have seen the pallor which a
whisper can bring upon the cheeks of hundreds. I
know that a casual rumor has again and again deprived
whole towns of a week's sleep. Negro insurrection is
the name for every horror, simply because it is one of
which the Southerners know nothing. It is doubtful
whether, in all the insurrections in the South for a hundred years put together, five hundred slaves have been
in actual insubordination. The present generation has
seen nothing of the kind. That is the very reason why
there is such a horror and panic about it : it is a vague,
mysterious, and unknown evil. As far as the shudder
about " covering the South with the horrors of insurrection " is real, and not a traitorous pretence, it may
be met by the fact that the history of insurrection
throughout the world shows that in every case the bar-
barity was chiefly on the part of the whites, and always
provoked by them. In every case, twenty blacks have

been butchered to one white. Of all the races now on earth, there is none so little cruel, so little bloodthirsty, as the negro; that being why it has been for so many ages the enslaved race. The only dread we could have in an immediate emancipation of this race is, that the Confederate forces would rush home to massacre their negroes. Doubtless they would ask the United States for a few months' truce for that purpose, — and as the family of fools is yet quite large and respectable, and most of them have managed to become generals in our army, there would be danger that our courteous McClellans, Hallecks, &c. would be " quiet " until the massacre should take place. But when we are up to such a master-stroke of justice, we shall be up to stripping the epaulets from negro-hounds and placing them on the shoulders of men. We should recognize in that call for a truce, which would surely come, God's invitation for us to march into the South the protectors of black and white, — an army of saviours, not of destroyers, — our glorious task to see that the transition-pangs of the South were safely passed, and her people born into light and liberty.

Let none doubt that the slave is ready to stir in a way which will paralyze the armies of the South, as soon as he hears the true voice. I once asked a slave why it was that he and others did not escape: he replied, " Because, after getting out of the slave-*holding* States, we must either drive under or fly over all the slave-*hating* States from here to Canada." Let Canada be carried wherever our flag goes ; nay, let every slave be empowered and authorized to make the spot on which he stands Canada.

The South has not a misgiving that her slaves are not generally asleep to these issues. I have heard of a Southerner who, having a Northern visitor before whom he was showing off Slavery in clean linen, finally alleged that his slaves were so happy that nothing could induce them to accept their freedom. To make the experiment perfect, he, in the presence of the Northern man, offered them their freedom if they desired to leave him. *Every one of them said he would accept freedom.* Whereupon the master swore at them as fools who did not know what was good for them, ordered them to their work, and in future exhibitions before Yankees never attempted the manumission-trick. Fortunately for him, the Yankee had already taken South-side views of the institution.

When John C. Fremont was a candidate for the Presidency there was no portion of the South where the watchword " Freedom and Fremont " was not heard at midnight. The South was on the verge of panic. Lately, when that same man was in the Western Department, that cry from the slaves was echoed from plantation to plantation all along the Mississippi, Tennessee, and Red Rivers ; and so frequent was it at last, that the apprehension reached the semi-loyal of the Tennessee and Kentucky border, who acted up through all the shades of disloyalty and loyalty, until the panic of rebels was felt at the Capitol, and removed the Warrior of Liberty from his command.

By that removal, and by the infamous proclamations and wanton renditions by which our officers have humiliated us even more than by their wretched incompetency, we have doubtless alienated these negroes from us. So that our task, at first easy, is now difficult. But it is certain that we need only let the slaves along the border know our good faith, to have the tidings flash through the South all along the lines of nature's telegraph; *the way to do this, is to free the slaves of the Border States immediately.*

When I first came North, I used to maintain stoutly, with my companions, that the slaves did not desire freedom. More than twenty years had I lived amongst those dumb creatures, never dreaming that any one of them had a thought of freedom. But when I returned South I found that they not only knew, what few whites knew, that I was antislavery, but they were eager to consult me as to how they might escape. All this took me by surprise; I had never hinted freedom to one of them, and it was in one of the obscurest parts of Virginia, where Northerners never came; then I saw, for the first time, that the whole social system of the South is undermined.

The South does not as yet fully comprehend her own weakness. But she knows that every warrior has his vulnerable heel. Our only danger is, that, before our slow Northmen are ready to act, the

South will suspect this her danger, and will cover it up with a decree of emancipation for all able-bodied men who will bear arms for the Confederacy. That would free nearly 500,000 negro men, which would be a cheap price to pay for a victory over the North, which would give them power to recover the emancipated half-million by reopening the slave-trade, and would not impair Slavery at all. (For I do not believe the South would give up Slavery for anything!) The children, by the codes of all slave states, follow the condition of the mother, and such a decree would manumit no women.

No bid that we could then make for these negroes would bring them to our side ; for they would then be under military rule, and animated by the spirit of the contest. The power that is nearest is that which they have most faith in ; a distant, less imposing power might double the offer with no effect.

There is one man in the South who has his eye steadily on the watch in this direction. Jefferson Davis has no faith whatever in the fondness of the negro for his condition.

A few years ago an artist of Philadelphia was engaged by the State of South Carolina to prepare some national emblematic picture for her State-House. Jefferson Davis was requested to act with the South Carolina committee in criticising the studies for this design. The first sketch brought in by the artist was a design representing the North by various mechanic implements, the West by something else, whilst the South was represented by various things, the centrepiece, however, being a cotton-bale with a negro upon it, fast asleep. When Jeff saw it he said, " Gentlemen, this will never do : what will become of the South when that negro wakes up ? "

The first blast from the trump of universal Freedom will reveal to Jeff and his Confederates that the negro has already waked up; also, which is more important, that the North is waked up; then will our army go marching on to bloodless victory, — trampling scourges, not men, breaking fetters, not hearts.

Ah, what tongue can celebrate a victory so glorious; a victory which would restore to our firesides the lost links of their circles ; which would touch the blighted lands of the South as by a magic wand, until its desert should rejoice and blossom as the rose ; which should clasp the broken arch between North and South with the infrangible keystone, eternal Justice !

VIII.

THE GRADUAL PLAN.

A Bohemian story relates, that Horace Greeley was lately travelling on a steamer, when a High-Church Episcopalian minister, who was on board, became much exercised concerning his (Greeley's) soul. At length this clergyman approached H. G., and, in a solemn voice, said, " Friend, may I inquire if you have ever been baptized? " " Well, no," replied Greeley, " not exactly; but I 've been vaccinated."

Gradual emancipation has about as much to do with putting down this rebellion through Slavery, as vaccination has with baptism.

The war power alone gives the President the right even to touch Slavery in the States with his little finger, as he has done; and the military advantage which he sees and assigns as a reason for his late proposition to co-operate in emancipation with slave States, is sufficient to justify abolition by the war power.

It is thus one of the Commander-in-Chief's guns; and to make it gradual would be like firing off a gun a little at a time, — if that were possible.

So far as emancipation will help us to crush this rebellion, no gradual plan which was ever conceived and tried can do us the least good. Any measure which leaves the slave bound at all to his Southern master, keeps him there adding to the wealth and support and military power of the hostile section. And if four millions of these laborers remain to furnish these supplies to the enemy, the South will be able to keep in the field all their white population, and, whatever advantages we may gain, their rebellion will survive the youngest person in this nation.

But, looking at the matter apart from the national emergency, and simply as a question of political economy, to say that gradual emancipation is better for all is to throw away all the light of experience in this matter. Negro slàves have within this century been emancipated in seven or eight countries. And if there is one thing in which all reports agree, it is, that wherever the thing was done in any half way, the country suffered in* exports and imports; wherever it was done cleanly, immediately, and unconditionally, the country never failed to reap a full and immediate reward. Whilst the island of Jamaica, under the gradual plan, groaned under its losses, the adjacent islands which made a clean sweep of Slavery saw their five talents at once swell to ten. Russia is now undergoing the same experience with its serfs, who, kept in limbo between Slavery and Liberty, have proved such a burden that the taskmasters are crying out to the Czar to have them given equal rights or none at all.

HOMER NODDING. I allude to the Rev. Homer Wilbur, of the Atlantic Monthly. Many a noble refrain of freedom, which lingers in our hearts in the watches of the night, which greets the rising day, must be traced to this Homer; but lately it would seem that his Muse threatens to reverse the story of Undine, and gradually lose her soul. What else can be said concerning his Polliwog fable? This fable compares those who would declare Slavery at an end, so far as this government is concerned, to those philotadpoles who, impatient at the slow growth by which Nature leads polliwog to frog, insisted on cutting off the tails of the former. After this Homer writes: "I would do nothing hastily or vindictively, nor presume to jog the elbow of Providence. No desperate measures for me till we are sure that all others are hopeless,—*flectere si nequeo* SUPEROS, *Acheronta movebo.*"

In other words, the slaughter at Manasses, Ball's Bluff, Winchester, Shiloh, are mild measures; these are appeals to the gods; but to release millions from dungeons, fetters, auction-blocks, and raise them to life, this is a "desperate measure," this is to "move hell"!

Is it possible that any cataract should have been so far formed over this once clear eye, that it now sees a state of Slavery to be a normal phase in the condition of human beings? O Homer, once you sang as if you saw that Slavery, and not emancipation, was the murderous lopping off of the poor polliwog's tail!

So far as the principle,

"From lower to the higher next,
Not to the top, is Nature's text,

is concerned, it is certainly true. Only, to apply it in

the present case as against immediate emancipation gives
an odd suggestion of a Sleepy Hollow somewhere near
Cambridge. Does Homer remember nothing of the
long and fearful years in which we have gone — God
knows how wearily and slowly — from step to step up
to this our Commencement-Day ? To speak of emancipation *now* as hasty, or a leap over essential steps, is as
if Homer should go to the next Senior who, having
made his graduation speech, at the end of a full Col-
lege course, is about to receive his diploma, and say :
" My dear young man, *festina lente !* You must n't
think of a diploma until you have been here four
years yet. Come over, — our Ollendorf class meets
at ten now."

Or here, say, is an old tree which has been slowly
rotting, until a breath only may bring it to the earth ;
now, merely because it falls with a crash, and the
splinters fly, shall we accuse the blithe breeze which
did the work of being a revolutionary tornado, moving
Acheron ?

Let us trust that Providence will " presume to jog
the elbow " of Homer, that he may no longer nod
whilst the first page in God's account with America
is closing, and when it is plain that upon the virtue
and earnestness of the current hour it must depend
whether there shall be any balance in favor of this
nation to be carried to the fresh page, or to entitle
it to further trust.

IX.

WAR FOR THE UNION.

WE are told, with a frequency and vehemence which so simple a proposition could scarcely be supposed to evoke, that "this is a war for the Union." We can account for the vehemence by the supposition that this sentence has a reverse side, which is, that "this is *not* a war for emancipation."

We do not need a war for emancipation. Slavery is the creature of positive law ; it is maintainable only by systematic force. Only withdraw the *positive supports* of Slavery, — only let the government declare that IT will henceforth ignore the relation of master and slave, — and Slavery falls by its own weight.

But has not this idea of a "war for the Union" its comic side ? I once knew of a father's whipping his child because the child did not love him so well as it did its nurse, and it seemed to me an odd way to cultivate filial affection ; but is it not so that we are recovering unity with the South ? If *that* Union had not been already dead, surely we have sent artillery enough down there to have killed it several times. Whether we shall succeed with our arms or not, it would be a corpse that we conquered, galvanize it as we might. My theory of General McClellan is, that he has just sense enough to see that, the object as-

signed being to restore the Union, the more he should
fight, the less Union he would have. He had probably concluded that harmony was more likely to come
by his sitting on the Potomac and waiting for it to
turn up ; and he might have been sitting there still
if the country had not been of a different opinion.

Andy Johnson goes to Tennessee, and pleads with
that people to see that the old Union is re-established
in that State, and his leading argument to them is
that Slavery, now in a precarious condition, will thereby be secured more firmly than ever. In the present
representative position of Mr. Johnson, we must conclude that our government would be only too happy
to clasp the broken arch with the old keystone which
has just crumbled. But there are two classes in this
country, either of which holds the balance of power,
which will take care that no such reunion takes place.
One class resides in the Cotton States. The Cabinet need never hold any love-feasts for Jeff and his
companions. In Ireland, where the priests pray over
the little fields of the peasantry to assist their fertil-
ity, a priest once came to a particularly barren and
hard-looking patch of ground, and said, " Brethren,
there's no use in praying here ; this needs manure."
I think when Father Abraham looks over the fence
of the Cotton States, if he ever does, he will come to
a similar conclusion about the efficacy of pardoning
grace. The other class which, should the South submit to-morrow, would prevent any return to the old

Union, is the class of honest freemen throughout the land. The battle of Armageddon is one that never ceases. Let the Cabinets at Washington and Richmond join again around the communion-table, with the blood of the Christ crucified between them upon it, — and the old siege of Liberty against the Union, which has been raised for a moment, begins again. Garrison, the old standard-bearer, will unfurl his banner of Disunion, which he keeps only tucked away in the Liberator room, as Bennett of the Herald keeps the Confederate flag. The clear bugle of Phillips sounds the old martial call again. And all along the sky sleeping thunders will awaken, and ten thousand trumpets proclaim that the siege against the ancient wrong is renewed, — the siege whose arrows are thoughts, whose shells are fiery inspirations of truth, whose sword is the Spirit of a just God. All this will go on until the ballot-box is conquered again, and some such man as Wendell Phillips is elected President. Then another Sumter gun will be heard. Then will come the war of which the present is but a picket skirmish. John Brown will be commanding general of all our forces then; and all will not be quiet on the Potomac. His soul will go marching on; 't is a way it has.

For I fear that over the eye of this nation Slavery has gradually formed a hard cataract, so that it cannot see the peace and glory which are an arm's-length before it, — a cataract which only the painful surgery of the sword can remove. If it be so, we can only say, — Bleed, poor country! Let thy young men be choked with their blood ; let the pale horse trample loving hearts and fairest homes; if only thus thou canst learn that God also has his government, and that all injustice is secession from that government, which his arm of might will be sure to crush out!

Those who oppose the method of emancipation allege that it would exasperate the South to the utmost, would alienate them forever from us, would unite the Border States with them, and unite them all against us as one man.

The fear of exasperating the South reminds one of the toper, who said that, when it got to be twelve o'clock of the night, he did not care *when* he went home ; for his wife was by that time as mad as she could be, and an hour or so made no difference. The South has about filled the gamut of wrath. Nor have we seen much difference in its treatment of such Southern pro-slavery men as General Anderson and his brother Charles, and antislavery men. So far as our experience in this war goes, they had as lief a man should be a Garrisonian as a Lincolnite.

So far as the objection relates to the supposition that an edict of emancipation would turn the Border States against us, it, being military, may easily be met as such by the fact that, even if a million people became estranged from us, (the very largest estimate,) such an edict would at once bring four million (the slaves) to our side. And mark the difference between those who would go and those who would come.

The million who went would prove by their going that they were pretended, or at least half-hearted, friends; they would show that their loyalty was but a cover for the preservation of Slavery, — that the Union meant for them nothing, if not human chattels. The four millions who would be riveted to our side by this one blow would be those upon whom we might depend, since their every possible interest would then be involved in our success. *Now*, it is the interest of the negro that the country should be divided, unless he is to be emancipated; for disunion would at least bring Freedom's southern line down to Mason and Dixon's.

The million who would abandon our cause would be chiefly on the border, within territory already under military occupation; their disaffection would only need a little more vigilance on our part, and that would be a wise thing in any case. The four millions who would be our determined co-laborers from that moment are chiefly in disloyal territory under rebel occupation; they are there where we are striving, by expensive and perilous expeditions, to carry Union men; and by being salable property they are protected as no other soldiers we could have there would be.

Thus, even so far as the two are of military importance, the emancipation method offers far more than the mere fighting method. But there is another force brought into the action by emancipation which would change this war of disunion into a putting forth of unifying energies, which would be as irresistible in establishing our social unity as are our mountains and valleys and rivers in establishing our geographical unity.

X.

HOW TO HITCH OUR WAGON TO A STAR.

IT is one of the signs of the times, that the revolution was strong enough to take up bodily the Sage of Concord, and set him in the capital of this nation to instruct our rulers. The advice he gave them may be summed up in the one sentence, *Hitch your wagon to a star!*

Why not, Mr. President! You have some difficulty in making things go, possibly have some doubt as to whether they can be made to go; but if you could manage to hitch the Union to a star, *that* will be sure to move. If you can get the LAWS OF NATURE to aid in the reunion of North and South, you need not fear any Confederate efforts at keeping them apart.

The very intensity and virulence of the hatred which the South has for the North suggest that the feeling

is extremely morbid, and not very deep. It is not
deliberate, nor based on any actual difference, and
for that very reason must make up in violence what
it lacks in the nature of things. This hatred also
has sprung up too quickly to have much depth or
genuineness. It was within a comparatively recent
period that the South was one with the North. We
are of the same blood; our fathers were within our
memory united. Section has intermarried with section.

There has been but one Satanic divider who has
opened a chasm between us, — Slavery. The interests
of Slavery cannot be made the interests of free society;
and there cannot be one institution of free society —
such as the free press, and free speech, and free school
— which is not a bomb-shell for Slavery. Free society
being necessarily a continual assault upon Slavery,
Slavery hates the North. It is not the Southern man,
it is the virus of Slavery in his veins, which hates the
North; as the Indian plead before the court, that not
he, but the whiskey, committed the murder. Take that
virus away, my Northern friend, and he is a Saxon
man, she a Saxon woman, like yourself.

The writer of these pages was reared in the midst
of hatred and contempt of the Northern people, and
did himself hate and despise them cordially during
all his early youth; he held it to be his highest ambi-
tion to assist in severing that section from the North.
But fortune led him to a year's residence in a little

Quaker settlement where Slavery did not exist, and which consequently was an oasis upon a Slavery-wasted desert; and with this one step out of the atmosphere of Slavery, with the first glance of doubt toward that institution, a cloud of illusions cleared up, the antipathy to Northern men disappeared, and he experienced a revulsion in their favor which did them even more than justice.

He knows, moreover, the leaders of the Southern Rebellion, many of them personally, all of them by character, and knows them to be very earnest madmen; he knows that the North can, by sealing up the one source of madness and disunion which has within a few years brought about this alienation, wither it up forever.

France and England had a much longer and more rancorous feud than this between the North and the South. " I will fight a Frenchman," said Lord Nelson, " wherever I can find him; wherever he can anchor, my ship shall be there." But a year of a common interest made them allies; lately their sovereigns exchanged visits; and it is the estimate of the best judges that the current generation will bear to its grave all memory of the feud between the English and the French.

Men will love, and if need be die for, that by which they and their families live. If Slavery is the basis of their homes; if from slave institutions comes the bread that sustains the life of wife and child, then they will fight and die for Slavery. If the home, the bread of wife and child, are derived from free institutions, then for these men will fight and die. Did we only compel the people of the South to get their daily bread from free institutions, in less than five years they would be ready to fight and die by our sides for free institutions. They would call the Yankees by hard names for some years after, no doubt, but there could be no war between the sections; on the contrary, every healing influence in the universe would be at work to cure these lacerations made by the tomahawk of Slavery, which would then be buried.

When Freedom folds her blessed wings over both North and South, then every steamer, every car, every telegraphic line plying between them, will be a shuttle ceaselessly weaving together the hearts of their millions into one woof of interest and affection.

But who can enumerate or utter one in a thousand of the unswerving, all-compelling laws with which those who trust in Everlasting Justice ally themselves: steadfast upon their orbits, my masters, these stars will surely move, and no Southern Sisera shall be a match for them in their courses. But we must hitch our cause to them: the Sage said, — We cannot bring the heavenly powers to us, but if we will only choose our jobs in directions in which they travel, they will undertake them with the greatest pleasure. It is a peremptory rule with them, that they never go out of their road.

XI.

THROUGH SELF-CONQUEST TO CONQUEST.

A GREEK fable relates, that when Hercules and Achelous fought together, Achelous changed himself into the form of a mad bull, thinking to contend more strongly; but Hercules retained the FORM OF A MAN, and, seizing the horn of the bull, it broke off in his hand, and became the celebrated cornucopia.

One very obvious interpretation of this fable is, that it is always best to take the bull by the horns. But I use it for the ancient testimony it conveys in favor of the superiority of the purely human power over the greatest animal ferocity.

How rarely has Slavery, in its violent advance, been met in the *manly* way; how much oftener by the fawning of hounds! And it is just this unmanly attitude which the representatives of the North have so long assumed that has invited the arrogant demands of Slavery which are now resisted with bloodshed. Mr. Goodall, of Cleveland, Ohio, under affidavit to prove John Brown's insanity, related that once, when on the cars with him, they fell into some conversation concerning Slavery, and in reply to some of Brown's radicalism, " I attempted," says Goodall, " to point out a more conservative course, remarking very kindly to him that Kentucky, in my opinion, would have been a free State ere this, had it not been for the excitement and prejudices engendered by ultra abolitionists of Ohio. At this remark, he rose to his feet, with clenched fist, eyes rolling like an insane man (as he most assuredly was), and remarked, that the South would become free within one year, were it not that there were too many such scoundrels as myself to rivet the chains of Slavery." Innocent Goodall of Cleveland! how little did you know that you were seeing a picture then which Art and Poetry will combine to celebrate as one of the first gleams of sanity out of a nation's long lunacy! That remark of Brown's is precisely the sanest I ever heard. If the North went South nobly, Slavery would clear away like a phantom of night. Whatever be the faults of Southerners, they do like those who stand up squarely for their principles; in all my life in the South, I never remember to have heard a dough-face in the North spoken of otherwise than with contempt.

Let me relate a conversation literally as it occurred a few years ago in Richmond, Virginia. Some New York lawyer had in the case of the Lemmon slaves, which involved a principle important to the South, argued the case successfully for Lemmon and Slavery. He then came down to Virginia to be lionized. A dinner was given in Richmond by persons connected with the Legislature, to which this lawyer was invited. Here is the conversation, just as it occurred across the table from the lawyer, between two members: —

1st Member. "I don't think much of that man."

2d Member. "Nor I."

1st Mem. "He is n't a gentleman; but it's well enough to have such men up North."

2d Mem. "They're useful enough."

1st Mem. "Tom, why is it they never raise any gentlemen up North?"

2d Mem. "O, I've been North, and I tell you they do have gentlemen; but then they're all damned Abolitionists."

Virginia said to Edward Everett, "I envy not the heart or the head of the man who, trained amid free institutions, comes down to defend Human Slavery";[*] to John Brown Virginia said, "He is firm, truthful, intelligent, — the gamest man I ever saw."[†]

Sitting, last summer, in the porch of a hotel at Newport, Rhode Island, I heard the original conversation between a Northerner and Southerner which W. Shakespere has travestied by premeditation in the following conversation between Hamlet and Polonius: —

"*Ham.* Do you see yonder cloud, that's almost in the shape of a camel?

"*Pol.* By the mass, and 't is like a camel, indeed.

"*Ham.* Methinks it is like a weasel.

"*Pol.* It is backed like a weasel.

"*Ham.* Or like a whale.

"*Pol.* Very like a whale."

The Hamlet in this case was a wealthy semi-

---

[*] John Randolph of Roanoke.   [†] Henry A. Wise.

Southerner, with Secession sympathies, thinly disguised
under a few star-spangled phrases ; the compliant Polonius was from Boston, — where the largest and the
smallest things are said and done of any place on this
continent. In Boston you shall find your noblest and
your meanest man ; there you shall find the faithful
Senator who will stand for Freedom until he is strick-
en down, and there the creature who will touch glasses
with the assassin of his own Senator within two squares
of the prostrate form. We had brutes enough in Cincinnati to mob Wendell Phillips ; but no man who
could write a sentence could be found here who would
justify it : the mob had to go to Beacon Street, Boston, for a defender ; the *Courier* was ready to do
their work ! But where else could we have found a
Phillips ?

But, to return, the conversation between the two
men in Newport, both persons of distinction, was exactly given in the extract from Hamlet. The Bos-
tonian atoned for saying that he favored the Union,
by allowing every noble idea and name of America,
and especially of his own State, to be vilified in his
presence.

When is this contemptible and cowardly abasement
to end ? Will the line of such poltroons hold out to
the crack of doom ? I add my testimony to that of
Miss Grimké, Mr. Helper, Mattie Griffith, and other
natives of the South who have caught a glimpse of
the monster, whose coils have been tightening about

the dear land they have been compelled to leave, and who are doing their utmost to rescue it; with them I declare, that I have known nothing so heart-sickening, so chilling, so utterly diabolical, as that which calls itself conservatism in the North.

When I first sat foot in New England, I met, at a table in Boston, the Hon. Mr. ———. Hearing that I was from the South, he instantly turned his attention to me, and began a series of adulations of Southern institutions and people; apologizing for his own region; sneering at the liberal men of New England, as a very small band of crazy folk! What deathly colds fell on me then I pray may never fall on him! Through how many toils and struggles had I come to rest upon the free heart of New England; by what weary marches and flinty paths had I come to do homage to those men at whom he was sneering, as to heralds of this nation's promised land! I turned, and told him plainly that he had mistaken my opinions, which were not those common in the South; and that I could not help thinking that such disparagements of free men and institutions, on the part of those whom they had fostered, were like tempting with alcohol an inebriate whose family is starving at home.

I have in my mind a case of a very different kind. It was, I believe, about eight years ago that I was consulted by a committee at New Haven as to whether I knew any gentleman in the South who would be

willing to deliver a lecture in New Haven in defence
of the institution of Slavery. My mind fixed upon
George Fitzhugh, of King George County, Va., who
had written works on the "Failure of Free Society,"
and "The Sociology of the South." Mr. Fitzhugh
went to New Haven, and gave, on the evening of his
arrival, a lecture entitled, "Free Society a Failure."
Wendell Phillips was present, and heard the lecture,
and Mr. Fitzhugh evidently took pleasure in seeing
him. Fitzhugh's method of proving Free Society a
failure was by theories and speculations which had
got into the crevices and under the eaves of his brain,
like the bats in the rickety old mansion, situated on
the fag-end of a once noble estate, in which he re-
sided. This spot of "the sacred soil" he had never
left for a month, and of Free Society, of course,
knew nothing. At New Haven he fell, I am happy
to say, into very different hands from those of the
Hon. Mr. —— of Boston, or of Polonius at Newport.
He was the guest of that honest and noble man, if
God ever made one, the late Mr. Samuel Foote. On
the next morning after the lecture, Mr. Foote took
Mr. Fitzhugh in a buggy, and drove throughout the
beautiful town of New Haven and its environs; showed
him houses and cottages which would be marvels of
elegance in Virginia, and informed him, without any
allusion to log-cabins, that many of these mansions
belonged to mechanics, and some even to day-labor-
ers. Fitzhugh was thunder-stricken. He had proved

Free Society a failure without ever leaving his State; nobody replied to him, but he went home answered. He always preserved an ominous silence about the visit; but he acknowledged his mistake about Northern society, and though before that he had invariably printed a pamphlet every six months in favor of the "Sociology of the South," I believe he has not penned a line of the kind since. The grave and impressive rebuke of Samuel Foote, who simply said that he "would take him (Fitzhugh) out to see how Free Society had failed," was never lost. Mr. Foote was a gentleman in an old sense, which is sometimes forgotten even in scholastic Boston; that is, he was *gentle*, but always *man*.

If Northern men would oftener refrain from abnegating their manhood and slandering their own country, — did they act this manly and gentle part toward Southern men, — I can imagine many benefits which must flow from such a course. The South would respect the North, and the sentiment of the North. The South always believed that the North would cringe to the last, as she had been doing for fifty years. What say you, gentlemen, are we done cringing? Or is Mr. Vallandigham and his posture to be first endured, then pitied, then embraced, — as, according to the poet, is the way with moral monsters? "I do not trust him," said Richelieu of the soldier; "he bows too low." Hamlet never despises Polonius more than when the latter fools him to the top of his bent. Had the North been determined, outspoken, and faithful to herself, she must have been faithful also to the South, and might have averted the tumor which now eats into her Southern brother's heart, instead of fostering it.

"What mighty matter," says the Brahmin, "is the subjugation of the sea-girt earth to those who cannot subdue themselves." Not until we have conquered this dapperness and inhumanity in ourselves; not until the North ceases to ask what shall be done with negroes; not until the infamy of Illinois Black Laws is held to be deeper than Carolina Slave Laws, — can we gain any noble victory. Through self-control lies the only path to control; at present we have as yet to prove that we are worthy to win the victories of Liberty and Law.

When the North rises fully to the stature of manhood, and grasps the sharp horn of the Southern Achelous with a human hand, — no longer meeting horn with horn, — then that horn will break off, and become for this nation the horn of plenty. A touch of pure humanity can make this Rebellion yield a fruitage of peace, prosperity, and honor for which we might otherwise have had to wait a century. Ah, had we a Hercules, knowing that hand is stronger than horn, to guide us!

XII.

A POST-PRANDIAL POINT.

AT a dinner given in Washington to Mr. Prentice, Mr. Secretary Smith, replying with warmth to some strong antislavery sentiments which had just been uttered by Mr. Cameron, said: "If we, being eighteen millions, cannot put down this rebellion of six millions without freeing their slaves, we ought to give the war up."

Doubtless the Secretary, when he got off this bit of wisdom, had been paying more attention to his own Interior than to that of the country.

Six bad men can burn up a half-dozen blocks of a city, and destroy a thousand lives, before they could be arrested. It would be a fine thing for such to retain at their trial Mr. Smith, whose opening position would be: " Gentlemen of the Jury, if several blocks of a city and hundreds of people cannot keep from being burnt up by six men, they ought to be burnt up!"

The remark brings before us the inequality of the combatants in this war.

Some years ago Daniel Webster was challenged to a duel by some booby from Texas, (I believe,) whose range of ability was limited to the skilful use of rifle and bowie-knife. Mr. Webster was inclined to accept the challenge; but his friends interfered, and declared that the stakes were unequal; that such a brain as that of Daniel Webster's could not be risked against even many hundreds of Texans, much less this boor. They were willing that a certain mad bull at Marshfield should meet the Texan, but compelled Mr. Webster to decline.

The reading public is now reading with delight the exquisite delineations of Theodore Winthrop. You who have read " Cecil Dreeme," " John Brent," and " Edwin Brothertoft," think a moment of such an imagination, such culture, being at the mercy of some wretched little drummer-boy! Where are his equals in the South? or those of Lyon, of Baker, or of Fitz-James O'Brien?

But these are minor inequalities, and we allude to them only to remember that there is a fearful inequality in the institutions which produce such men as those I have named, and those which produce Floyds and Twiggses in shoals, but to eight millions of men not one literary or scientific man of any importance.

Americans! we have no right to imperil LIBERTY one hour, nor to allow it to remain in peril, that we may show the world that we can " whip the South." The point which the Secretary of the Interior raised is but a point of sectional vanity, and it is far beneath the tremendous issue in this crisis. Is it a point of pride with Freedom to prove that it excels Slavery as butcher of men? When this war began, the successes were more frequently on the side of Slavery, and the wisest said : " There are glorious obstacles to the success of the North ! Free institutions do not breed the requisite number of Floyds and Twiggses — thieves and traitors — for this work ; Freedom's sons cannot hate and sting like vipers ; they will not poison springs, and put up false banners to lure a foe into traps." There *was* room for some pride in that direction. But these glorious obstacles are fading ; the thirst for Southern blood grows ; and presently the North will be demoralized enough to equal the recklessness and spite of Slavery.

Once, says a fable, there was a stag which had long, branching horns, of which it was very proud ; but of its feet it was very much ashamed. One day this stag, pursued by hounds, found its despised feet quite serviceable ; and indeed the feet would have saved him had it not been for the horns of which he was so proud, for these becoming entangled in some bushes, the stag was overtaken by the hounds.

The North can win no military laurels in this conflict ; should it gain the victory, the world will see as little glory in it as it saw in our victory over Mexico. Let the North not covet a distinction which she can never possess, thanks to the superior glories of Liberty ! To the proposition from South Carolina, that her sons should meet more than their number of Massachusetts men, and decide the issue in this country by this duel of States, a shrewd resident of the Old Bay proposed, as an amendment, that these should meet, but that, instead of using weapons of death, vast blank-books should be opened, and if a third more Massachusetts men could not write their own names than South Carolina men, the South should be declared victorious. That was rather cruel toward the Southerners, beneath whose rule, entirely great, the bowie-knife is mightier than the pen; but it was from a man who had wit enough to know that Liberty's Code of Honor is a different one from that of Slavery. To that or any legitimate weapon we may confidently trust American Freedom; but not one hour to the shifting chances of war, if we can help it, — not to the accident of a general's being drunk or sober, or the position of a ditch or fence. If these flimsy defences are the surest with which we can surround the world's trust to America, be sure the precious lamp will be removed to those who can keep it alive, though we be left in outer darkness.

XIII.

THE PROBABILITIES OF INSURRECTION.

THE experience of the Slave States has furnished reason to believe that no general and concerted insurrection of slaves can occur for many years.

In estimating this question, several things are to be

remembered : — 1. That the negroes cannot generally write, or use the mails or the facilities of travel. They are undoubtedly anxious enough for their freedom to strike any blow that might have a reasonable prospect of success ; but they can see as readily as we that concert would be necessary, and that to any great extent is impossible. It will be remembered that the insurrection of Nat Turner and that planned by Denmark Vesey covered very small sections of the States in which they occurred, though they were the most extensive and elaborately prepared of all that have occurred. 2. The negroes are an extremely cautious people, and not at all self-reliant. Much of this is the result of their training. A negro may be browbeaten even into the confession of things he has not done ; and at a word of suspicion about any real offence, he at once supposes the master knows everything, and makes a clean breast of it. It is probably through these means, rather than deliberate treachery upon the part of any of them, that schemes of this kind have been so often betrayed by negroes themselves. 3. The negroes are superstitious, and in the direction of special providences. They believe generally in luck and miracle, and the fatalism of the Baptist Church, to which they usually belong, helps to cut the sinews of their own right arms. " Who would be free, themselves must strike the blow," would be an incomprehensible sentiment among them, and, in my opinion, it will never be true in their case. When their blow comes, it will be at the end of a long series of others' blows. They are always looking for their Moses, whom they would not follow unless he had his wonder-working rod along. 4. But the chief fetter worn by this race is the habit of servile obedience : the master's ordinary tone and cowhide are more irresistible than his musket and epaulets.

Undoubtedly there will be in the future, as there have been in the past, here and there local insurrections ; but none that could excite a general panic in the South will this generation be apt to witness.

On reflection, it will be seen that all of the forces above enumerated as those which will be likely to prevent any general slave insurrection are at the present time doubly active. In the present juncture, the slave has every inducement to remain quiet, none at all to rebel : neither side is ready to befriend him as an insurrectionist, both are helping him as a slave. He is, of the three parties in this contest, as he should be, infinitely the best off. At any rate, he is very sure not to rebel when every Southern eye is on the watch, and every hand on the trigger.

So those who are hoping to have their shoulders relieved of the burden of doing justice to these slaves will find that they will act as Paul and Silas when their prison was opened by an earthquake, who said to the frightened Macedonians, " Let the magistrates come and fetch us out." He certainly will not stir to befriend or welcome those who have not decided whether or not to exile him in case he becomes free ; who have not yet declared even those deserted by rebel masters to be free ; and who really show more aversion to personal proximity to him than his Southern master.

But every one of the *inward* links which bind him now — his caution, superstition, and servile obedience — would be transferred to our banner on the instant that he should be declared free under it, and would curl about it like tendrils. Not insurrections, but stampedes, would at once follow our proclamation of freedom ; and they would have to be, and would be, checked immediately. But to check them knocks into *pi* every column of the Southern army.

The slave's heart everywhere is at this moment filled with the one burning idea of freedom ; he is doing now exactly what his friends advise him to do, — sitting still ; he has shown great wisdom during this war. But he listens every hour of the night and day for the watchword which calls him to his feet.

That word is not Confiscation ; it is not Colonization. Hearing people discussing and advocating every measure for these people except simple justice, one thinks of Cassim, loaded with treasures in the robbers' cave, with the door fast locked in his face, calling for it to open by every name but the one to which it really does open. He says, " Barley," and " Oats," — but the door opens not a crack. Let our rulers take care that the Sesame which alone can open the door of success in this war is not first uttered, as in Cassim's case, by the robbers : the side that first cries FREEDOM TO THE SLAVE gains the day in this war.

We hear some talk of arming the slaves: would it not be well first to try the effect of doing them simple, unelaborate justice?

For that word the slave's heart far down on the Southern plantations is now all ear. It is a common error to suppose that the slaves on the plantations of the far South are more ignorant, degraded, and obtuse, or that they are less informed in public matters, than those in the Border States. The contrary is truer. It has been for many generations the invariable custom to send to these plantations of the Cotton and Sugar States every negro near the border who at any time shows a desire for freedom, or who has attempted to run off, or has been overtaken, or who shows enough intelligence for an inference that he will be restive under the yoke. The number of overseers and strictness of patrol on these plantations make it comparatively unimportant whether the slave is discontented or otherwise. The consequence is, that there has been through many years a gradual accumulation in the far South of the most inflammable and intelligent negroes; and any serious insurrections would be far more apt to come from them than from their more comfortable Border-State comrades.

But they listen on the Border also for that word to whose Orphic music the hearts of men are made to dance, though they were as stones and trees. The

Border-State negro has had his senses whetted by a
certain kind of perpetual fear and ever-recurring
anguish. For these are the slave-breeding States. Not
one half of the slaves born in any of the Border
States are or can be retained there; the demand for
them is insufficient. This makes the yoke through
all this region terribly galling. Year by year parents
watch the growth of their children, knowing that they
cannot be kept at home, — that there each will be only
another mouth to feed and back to clothe, — knowing
that so soon as the year of noblest promise and strength
comes, it comes only to bring the bitter parting and
heart-break. No farmer gathers in his harvest more
regularly than the slave-trader of the Border States,
putting in his scythe this year for the human hearts
which were not quite ripe for plantation-service last
year.

Thus they listen, thus they watch, more than they
that watch for the morning: God's captive Israel, of
whom he says, They shall prosper who love thee!

XIV.

MERCY, AND NOT SACRIFICE.

AFTER what has been said, there is no need that we shall dwell upon the objection, sometimes offered to an edict of emancipation, that it would cover the South with a cruel servile insurrection.

Even if it were true, the objection is absurdly oblivious of the cruel white insurrection which is now raging in the South, to say nothing of its ignoring the chronic and perpetual insurrection against the rights and happiness of a whole race, which Slavery essentially is.

But the history of every nation which has dared the guilty experiment of holding man as property repeats the warning of Schiller, — " Tremble before the man who has not yet broken his chain: tremble not before the freeman."

Though no insurrection of slaves can possibly come to do for us in this war what an edict of emancipation alone can do ; though for a generation, or generations, the slave may serve his Southern master; yet, if that institution be allowed to survive this war, the South is delivered up as to the ever-narrowing circles of a whirlpool, which must bear it into its vortex, unless another war may once more give the nation the power to rescue that insane section. For these slaves must multiply until their enslavement becomes impossible. Any man, whose opinion is entitled to be listened to, knows that this institution is in the end a doomed institution. But we know, also, that slaveholding, like any other bad passion, grows with what it feeds on, and has thus been a more determined thing in the South with every successive year. If, then, in this Golden Hour, when we have the means already prepared and ready to prevent any evils which could occur, we do not, what is there in the future but a certain fearful looking for of judgment and fiery indignation ?

Are you quite sure, O ye who are so fearful of servile insurrection, that, at any other period, if the South shall cry, Help, — *as she surely will*, — we shall have a million men ready on the instant to shield her from carnage ?

The social system of the South has been undermined by the hand of God: when, in eternal wisdom and truth, he laid the foundations of the world, he loved the human being for which all was a mansion too well to permit any wrong to go on without retribution ; and under the foundations of all injustice he laid the trains which must in some way lay them in ruins. The fusee to that undermining is now in our hand : we may now fire it with fire from the altar of God, which can work no indiscriminate ruin ; but who shall tell the horrors if in the future that fusee shall be set on fire of hell ?

Nothing is more sad than when the human mind puts darkness for light, and light for darkness; and I know of no case where it is done more dangerously than in calling that measure inhuman and cruel which is the only one not utterly pitiless to the South.

The present attitude of the North *is* oppressive toward the South. The North seems disposed simply to cripple and limit Slavery, and yet about as anxious as the South to prevent emancipation. In other words, the North is opposed to freeing the slaves, but wishes so to limit the institution that it shall be a burden and a loss to those who hold it. For if the principles upon which the present President was elected should prevail, and the slaves not freed, the institution would utterly impoverish the South; and the North would be enriched by it. It is our duty either to liberate the slaves, or else to allow Slavery such protection and admission into all territories as will keep it from being a danger and a drag upon the South. I fear the North is anxious to preserve Slavery for the cotton and sugar it brings; but anxious also to have all the lands and political power, without which Slavery makes every white man as well as black man in the South a slave.

You have no right to leave this tree on their lot girdled, so as to bear them no fruit, and be in their way, and an increasing danger also, rotting year by year for the blast under which it shall fall suddenly and inevitably.

My fellow-men, there is every sign that our arms

are steadily winning their way into the South. Let us consider gravely *what it is* we are carrying South as we march on. One thing we must carry,—devastation. We are far yet from the heart of the South, and they know little of the South who do not know that, as we approach nearer, the tragedy will deepen : our army will mark its track in blood, and find ashes where fair cities stood before. Now I do not say that all this ought not to take place if it is necessary ; there are things worse than such devastation; but I do say that in .this age of the world such devastation of human homes and hearts cannot be justified unless along with it we bear blessings greater than the devastation is evil.

In my opinion, there is not a feature of Christianity which would not frown upon the idea that the sorrows which our victorious advance must bring upon the South can be justified by carrying a piece of bunting down there, or the mere governmental authority it represents. If this should prove to be, what Earl Russèll declared it, "a struggle for power" only, the verdict of the civilized world will be,— *Shame!* Take any one who perished at Fort Donelson, loyal or rebel, and place that human being, with God's crown of intelligence upon his brow, beside that mass of stone and brushwood which was surrendered, and any thinking person will know which is of more importance, the mass of brute matter which human hands could rear in a month, or that immortal being of heart and brain, which, once prostrated, not the combined skill of the world can rebuild.

The proverb says, "Faithful are the wounds of a friend"; and if we were smiting the South to heal her of the withering curse that is upon her, our wounds will be far more friendly than all those weak compromises and indulgences by which the North has for years helped to fasten her curse upon her. An amnesty for the South leaving her Slavery would be the bitterest wrong and cruelty we could inflict on her.

Humanity, Christianity, would welcome and justify any severity necessary to relieve the South of that curse, as they would the severity of the surgeon's probe, for the overbalancing benefit it brings. The friend of humanity could then patiently see more bloodshed than the land has yet witnessed, if he knew that this blood was shed for the remission of the nation's sin, the removal of its pitiless curse.

And yet, what are we actually carrying South with our arms? After the surrender of Fort Donelson, the first thing done was to run up the United States banner; the second thing was to return to rebel masters twelve slaves found therein. This was boasted of by a Kentucky Senator in the Senate, and the author of the deed went unrebuked. But we got through him at Shiloh as heavy a blow as those twelve negroes got. We shall find that all the orders "No. 3" will come home to roost. At Port Royal a negro, deserted by his master, came within our lines, and, addressing Colonel Lee, said, "Will you please, sir, tell me if I am a freeman ? " Colonel Lee was dumb. The government is dumb.* As yet you, my countrymen, are dumb.

Whatever title the Southern States may have had

* The following touching lyric was placed in my hand, soon after hearing of this incident, by one who has already given us that which is worthy to be incorporated with the "John Brown Song," as the "Battle Hymn of the Republic."

Tell me, master, am I free ?
  From the prison-land I come,
From a wrecked humanity,
  From the fable of a home, —

From the market where my wife,
  With my baby at her breast,
Faded from my narrow life,
  Rudely bartered and possest.

Masters, ye are fighting long,
  Well your trumpet-blast we know :
Are ye come to right a wrong ?
  Do we call you friend or foe ?

Will ye keep me, for my faith,
  From the hound that scents my track ?
From the riotous, drunken breath,
  From the murder at my back ?

God must come, for whom we pray,
  Knowing his deliverance true ;
Shall our men be left to say,
  He must work it free of you ?

Links of an unsighted chain
  Bound the spirit of our braves ;
Waiting for the nobler strain,
  Silence told him we were slaves.

to hold slaves, no man has yet been bold enough to claim that the United States has a title to hold them; yet it is restraining of their freedom thousands of men as free as the President. The President has just imported a million slaves into the States of Georgia, Florida, and South Carolina. A pretty big beam, I think, the Northern eye is carrying, as it goes to pull out the mote in the Southern eye! Buchanan announced that the Constitution carries Slavery wherever it goes: it has remained for the first Republican government to make the theory fact. But is to do this worth the heart-breaks, the butchery, by which alone we can march South?

————

XV.

THE CONSECRATION OF HEROISM.

IN the old Hebrew Chronicles it is related that, on one occasion, David was in an hold, and the garrison of the Philistines was in Bethlehem. "And David longed, and said, O that one would give me drink of the water of the well of Bethlehem which is by the gate! And the three mighty men brake through the host of the Philistines, and drew water out of the well of Bethlehem, that was by the gate, and took it, and brought it to David; nevertheless he would not drink thereof, but poured it out unto the Lord. And he said, Be it far from me, O Lord, that I should do this; is not this the blood of the men that went in jeopardy of their lives? Therefore he would not drink it."

Thus to all noble minds heroism is forever consecrated, and consecrates all it touches. The commonest things have a new and higher value, when they become associated with deeds of devotion and courage. The cross, to which the Christian world clings, was not a whit more respectable than a gallows, until a Hero's blood consecrated it.

Our countrymen, our companions, friends, and relatives, have gone forth, in jeopardy of their lives, to recover for this nation certain forts, arsenals, territories, — for which the nation longed. This nation does not yet see that when these forts and States are recovered for us, stained with the ruddy blood of thousands of its noble youth, — each the monument of fallen heroes, — they will seem very different from forts and arsenals; that, if thus recovered, they will be altars consecrated to the humanity which died to rescue them, flaming with the fires of Justice and Liberty.

The first American Revolution began as a protest against a tax upon tea and a few other articles. Even after Concord and Lexington the removal of a few pence from the duty on tea would have stopped the war. At this distance that looks to us as a very insignificant fight: one might almost call it a tempest in a tea-pot.

But so did it not remain. The tea reddened with the blood of noble hearts, as did the water of Bethlehem when it came to the king. Battle after battle came; men went on to death as to their beds; and from the fires of war emerged the grand figure of Independence. Then all the duties might have been taken off, but America would not have drank to the health of a tyrant what had now become the blood of her noble sons; nothing less than entire independence was worthy so costly a libation.

In the month of August, 1776,* immediately after the defeat of the Americans on Long Island, and whilst that disaster was not only demoralizing the army under Washington, but spreading dismay and consternation among the most resolute of the advocates of Independence, General Howe, wishing to take advantage of the terror which victory inspires, and persuading himself that the Americans, disheartened by so many checks, would be more modest in their pretensions, despatched General Sullivan to Congress, with a message purporting that, though he could not consistently treat with that assembly in the character they had assumed, yet he would gladly confer with some of their members in their private capacity, and would

---

* This incident was briefly alluded to in " The Rejected Stone "; the number of inquiries which have been made of me concerning it, and its appropriateness to the argument of this chapter, encourage me to condense the account from Carlo Botta's History, in which alone I have been able to find it, though it is certainly one of the most striking of our Revolutionary records.

meet them at any place they would appoint. He informed them that he was empowered, with the Admiral, his brother, to terminate the contest between Great Britain and America upon conditions equally advantageous to both. He assured them that, if they were inclined to enter into an agreement, much might be granted them which they had not required. He concluded by saying, that, should the conference produce the probability of an accommodation, the authority of Congress would be acknowledged, in order to render the treaty valid and complete in every respect. To this Congress made answer, through General Sullivan, that the Congress of the Free and Independent States of America could not, consistently with the trust reposed in them, send their members to confer with any one whomsoever, otherwise than in their public capacity. But that, as they desired that peace might be concluded upon equitable conditions, they would depute a committee of their body to learn what proposals they had to offer. The Deputies appointed by Congress to hear the propositions of the British Commissioners (General Howe and Admiral Lord Howe) were Benjamin Franklin, John Adams, and Edward Rutledge, all three zealous advocates of Independence. The interview took place on September 11th, on Staten Island, opposite Amboy, where the British general had his head-quarters.

The result of the interview showed to what a height the war, which began about a paltry tax, had risen under the tuition of Heroism. The British commanders offered every concession, with complete amnesties and indemnities, *provided only that they would lay down their arms and submit to the authority of England.* But the Americans, staggering though they were under a disastrous defeat, — dark, too, as was the prospect of three millions fighting against the strongest power on earth, — utterly and firmly refused to submit to anything less than their entire independence.

This was England's last effort to settle the difficulty by negotiation. Immediately thereafter she put forth her whole strength to compel submission : but had England only known it, she was conquered already, when in the midst of darkness and disaster there remained to confront her a spirit too noble to compromise Liberty, too royal to cool even the fevered lips of war with an ignoble peace, and offer to Despotism the blood of heroes.

Our public speakers know very well that, in speaking of " the Union cemented by the blood of our fathers," they touch a chord in the popular heart which never fails to respond. That is because it is a true chord. Every river and valley of it has been touched with the chrism of self-sacrifice.

But here is more blood poured out : what will that cement ? Is it only to cement the broken walls of Sumter ? Is it only to recover a section for freemen to be tarred and feathered in, — a Congress for honest Senators to be assassinated in ? Is that what your son has gone to cement with his blood? Are we giving up the best blood in our land that our flag may again unfurl its heaven-born colors for the protection of the chain and the lash and the block where immortal beings are sold as cattle?

There is where we started: the old Union just as it was, with every chain in it, every shamble, every scourge, every barbarism, — that is what our own valiant men brake the ranks of the Philistines to get for us. But already things give signs of change. People are saying, This war will be sure to end Slavery, — the wish being father to the thought. That is only the first flush on the water. Let us see a little more heroic blood shed, and people will say, This war *shall* end Slavery.

A man who announces — and this is said with all deference to the Secretary of State — that a bloody revolution shall sweep over a country, and leave that country, and every human being in it, in the same condition as before, must be in the counsel of that highly conservative angel at the Creation who was seized with a dreadful apprehension lest the very foundations of Chaos should be unsettled.

To expect that this revolution, whilst working changes similar to those which revolution has wrought in all history, will leave Slavery *as it was before* in the land, is to expect a conflagration enveloping a house to burn up the stone and iron, and leave the wood-work standing.

XVI.

A POSSIBLE BABYLON.

WHO can misread or doubt the prophecies written broadly over all the mountains, prairies, savannahs, lakes, and rivers of this superb continent? What heart can have a misgiving that these grandeurs have been prepared for a race of slaves? Does Niagara thunder of the great era of slave-coffles? Does the Mississippi suggest a race of clay-eaters on its shores? Do the great rivets between North and South, the Rocky, the Alleghany, the Blue Ridge mountains, foretell that the rivets of moral and political union on this continent are to be perpetual fear on one side and menace on the other, as they have been for years, — a union crumbling through very rottenness?

Every hill-top in America is a Pisgah, from which can be seen the Promised Land of Liberty, which this nation is sure sooner or later to enter.

But meanwhile there are dreary forty-year wanderings in desert places, which may have to come ere we are worthy to enter our Canaan of Freedom and Prosperity. Worse than all, there is a possible Babylonish captivity toward which it were well for this generation anxiously to look. The fearful retribution which befell Israel for its idolatry is never absent from the paths of such nations as turn aside from their own God to worship alien idols. Slavery is for this nation the alien idol, and its worship may yet have to be burnt out of us by a similar fiery trial.

There is a current phrase which says, " This war is bound to be the death of Slavery." It seems to me a very thoughtless speech. How do we expect emancipation to come ? Is it to be as a shower of gold ? The proverb says, " What will you have, quoth God ; pay for it and take it." We shall have freedom from our national curse, not by any luck, but when we are up to paying the fair price ; if there is enough humanity and common sense in the country to destroy Slavery, it will be destroyed, and not otherwise. No doubt Slavery will end, but this government may never live to see the day.

We actually hear people saying, " When this war is ended, we can have a convention, and agree upon some plan for the gradual abolition of Slavery."

When this war is ended ! This is much as when Paddy, after vainly endeavoring to put on a pair of new boots, remarked that he feared he would never be able to get those boots on until he had worn them a day or two.

Perhaps the highest secret which the Oriental philosophy hit upon was the peristaltic movement of the universe. The idea was that the visible universe was the integument of a great living soul, and that, in its onward progress, the vital form from time to time shed, as a snake its skin, this integument, whose spots were galaxies.

As long as the skin is alive and adjusted to its movement, the snake bears it onward; but when a newer one has been formed underneath, the snake pauses, contracts, and the old skin shrivels; one full-length stretch, and it is left in the path.

Onward by the perfect law the living essence of Society moves also: the customs, creeds, institutions, of any age are the spots of its variegated skin. Bright and beautiful are these scales when vital and necessary. Presently they get rusty, and must be shed. Then all the living forces contract, and the old is cast. *Nothing not dead can ever be sloughed off.* Revolutions such as Christianity, Protestantism, that which secured American Independence, that which is now abolishing Slavery, are the successive shrivellings of the rusty cuticle, as the living body of Society moves onward.

The former status of this country can never be restored, more than a snake can creep back into and inhabit the skin it has shed on the way-side. But, reader, have you not in your life found some poor snake still partially fettered to its "body of death," — snake in motionless distress, which, having stretched out from its shrivelled skin, must needs stretch back and wait? The last state of that snake is worse than the first for a time.

In this revolution we may get free. But if we do not, before any truce comes, cast the old Slavery-skin of this nation, we shall go back for a while into a state of things which even the Democrats would shudder to behold. If, now that Slavery and Freedom are, by the new power opened, for the first time left to the choice of the American people, they shall deliberately select Slavery, Slavery they will get with a vengeance! For things would have to be worse to be better. We should witness a rule of Slavery so galling and fearful, that the North would be scourged into a revolution.

There is no St. Patrick who can rid this land of old-line Democrats. Now and then there is a cry that the Democratic party is dead; and if it were not in league with the Devil, if bullets could kill it, it would have been dead long ago. In a play called "The Vampyre," the voracious sucker in human shape, who draws the life out of fair virgins whilst they sleep, is repeatedly slain; but in dying he always makes a pathetic request to have his corpse put at some certain place, — a place where the moonlight will, he knows, fall upon it. Whenever the moonlight touches this Vampyre in human shape, he revives. Now, this moonshine — which is a compromise between night and day — is a fair symbol of that which never fails to resuscitate Democracy. No matter how dead you may fancy it, you have only to heed its last dying request for a compromise, and under that moonshine its resuscitation is inevitable.

The very delay in dealing with Slavery has furnished sufficient moonshine, not to say lunacy, to stir the

Vampyre with a throb of life. That party is preparing
to go before the people in the forthcoming campaign.
They will take the Van Wyck Report in one hand, and
the Washburne Report in the other, (for they know how
to make the truth lie like the Devil!) and they will
say, from every stump in the country: "Feller-citizens! What did you git by leaving the old Dimocratic
party? Fust, you got a civil war, plunging into fraternal fratricide the country that under Frank Pierce
and Jim Buckhannon was peaceful, united, gellorious,
and happy. Second, you got untold millions of debt.
Third, you got corruption enough in all the branches of
the government to fill these here 2,000 pages of investigating reports. That's what you got by this Republican freak of yours! Feller-citizens, do you want to see
the bloody clouds of civil war roll away before the
rising sun of harmony and union, one and inseparable
now and forever? Jest vote for the regular nominees
of the Dimocratic party! Now, boys, three cheers
for McClellan!"

I fear the appeal will be successful; and if so, the
little finger of the man so elected will be heavier than
Buchanan's loins.

The other day I was reading in the Satanic Press
the programme of the Democracy, of which the above
is a free translation, and its editorial concluded with
saying, — "To this appeal the masses will be sure to
respond." By a typographical error, or the correc-
tion of some shrewd printer, the *m* got off of *masses,*

and on to the preceding word; and so it read "*them asses* will be sure to respond." It was very bad grammar, but I think I never read so sensible a sentence in that paper before. It is not the masses, but them asses, that we have to fear.

Let us not trust the sham Democracy of this country because it now professes to support the war. The other evening, when, at a Democratic meeting in Cincinnati, the corpse of the Vampyre was stirred, the assembly gave vent to the natural disgust by simultaneously ejaculating, *Pugh!*

Much to our surprise, an individual whose name is so pronounced, supposing himself called upon, made a speech. The Hon. George E. Pugh is the ablest Democrat in the West, and would so stand with his party if he were not a trifle too rash. When traitors in the West propose to aid the rebellion, they first inquire if Lawyer Pugh is in good health; and in so many cases of this kind has he appeared, that it is not strange if he should be in party limbo. But since Garrett Davis menaced the government with resistance from Kentucky, the sham Democracy of the West has come far enough out to lay hold upon Pugh.

At the assembly of Resurrectionists to which I have referred, this ex-Senator said these words: —

"The Democracy has voted men and money to support this government during the war; and the reason why they have done so is, that they have intended to have that government in their own hands at the next administration. In my opinion the government will soon be in the hands of the Democracy, and then, *and not till then*, will the old flag, with its thirty-four stars, represent a perfect Union."

That is, the Democracy, though not regarding the government, under a constitutionally-elected Republican administration, as a *bona fide* affair, will yet support it so long as there lingers with them a hope of binding the Union as a dead Hector to the chariot of Slavery.

" You aristocrats," says a Jacobin in Paris, " are frightened, as you say, lest we should injure your property : we shall guard your property with the utmost care, in the full expectation that it is soon to be our own."

But the proprietors knew that behind each of these words was a sword and a torch, and that, when it became certain that the Jacobin could not get the property, his sword and torch would appear.

The people are to be reverenced, but cautiously. When you can get a real people, their voice is the voice of God ; nay, when they are animated with a great, all-compelling purpose, they are the myriad-fingered hand of God, fashioning the Earth according to the pattern shown in the mount.

But from this height there is a precipitous descent. The people may be demoralized ; then they are not a people, but merely the rabble. Fearfully easy and swift is this recoil sometimes. To-day they sing Hosanna, and spread their garments in the path before the advance of the Highest; to-morrow the same voices sharply cry, Crucify him!

This Vampyre whom they would elect would fasten upon this nation, and suck every free and noble drop out of its heart. The sacred guaranties of Liberty and forms of law would be suspended then, not for the defence of Freedom, but to crush out the soul of Freedom. Slavery would be the tyrant, and dungeons would be filled with those who uttered a word or did aught against Slavery. Those weapons of martial law, far more fearful than any artillery, may each be wheeled around against the champions of Freedom; and there are men not very far from a possible Presidency who would use them all to strangle free thought and free speech in this country.

The Babylon whose captivity we have to fear is not Disunion; if that were the alternative, it would not be so fearful. But there are too many indications that the people of the North so worship the Union, and regard their trade as so involved in it, that, if they cannot win it by fair means, they will by foul. There is no doubt but they will fight and suffer long and gallantly to recover the Union; but when it is decided that they cannot have it with honor, it is to be feared that they can be demoralized enough to pay the price of their honor, to compromise for it.

But this would only be a thorny, crooked way to the same goal, the straight way to which God opens before

us to-day. It would not be long before the very men
who now think that they would be willing to have the
Union with Slavery in it back again, would shriek out
Anathema Maranatha upon every man who had a hand
in such a result.

XVII.

THE DIAL OF GROWTHS.

In the Palais-Royal Gardens at Paris there is a dial,
with a small cannon attached. When the sun rises to
the meridian height, the cannon is fired, a sun-glass
having been so arranged as to concentrate the rays for
that purpose.

Not far from this is another dial, arranged on the
same principle with the celebrated one made by Lin-
næus at Upsal: flowers there are which close, and
others which unfold, at various periods of the day, and
thus the hours are marked.

Thus the same sun which in one spot announces its
ascent to the zenith by the cannon's roar, in another
noiselessly traces its progress and culmination by the
closing up of old and the unfolding of new growths.

Ideas, sun-like, have also their dawn, their ascent,
and their culmination. One world lies about us where

ideas proclaim their advance through the grim mouth of the cannon. Powers, parties, interests, have so set their glasses, that fiery Liberty, vivifying Equality, radiant Fraternity, rising, dawn over dawn, upon the world, are responded to by the roar of battle. But softly about us lies another world, in which advancing Truth traces its steps of light in the closing up of old errors and the unfolding of new truths.

From the noisy thunders of the cannon-dial, — from the din of the voices which cry, Lo here! Lo there! — let us turn for a while, and trace so far as we can the hour as it stands in that kingdom which cometh not with outward show.

The leaders and masses enlisted in the Southern rebellion have no more to do with that rebellion than the *fantoccini* of a puppet-show have to do with their own attitudes and dances.

The present attitude of Slavery is the direct and inevitable result of the attitude of Liberty. The Satanic press throughout the country implores that the antislavery agitators shall be sent to Fort Warren; Parson Brownlow wishes to bury them in a ditch; the allegation being, that they have caused the rebellion, and are making a union after the old pattern impossible. Now, this is about as far as the Devil ever sees. He is shrewd enough up to a certain limit; after that he is as blind as a bat. It is as certainly true that antislavery agitation caused this rebellion, as that Slavery caused that agitation. It were easy to name one hundred brains which have been set a-thinking in this country during this generation, and to say with truth, if God had only seen fit to keep these hundred brains out of the world, or to have consulted Kentucky as to how he should fashion them, there would have been no war now. We should have gone on enjoying our country, our cotton, sugar, and the rest, as happy a nation of maggots as ever swarmed in an old cheese.

In the eyes of those who have a doubt whether that kind of life constitutes the whole duty and chief end of man, the Abolitionists can desire no fairer laurel for their brows than that through them streamed such fiery rays of Liberty, that Slavery had no choice but to close up like a deadly flower before unfolding Justice, or else respond to these noonday fires with the cannon. The "Rebellion Record" reports that the first gun of this war was fired last year at Charleston: the Muse of History will write that the first gun was fired by William Lloyd Garrison in Baltimore, many years ago; the shell he touched off was a long time on its way, and only lately exploded in the election of President Lincoln, who was sent to Washington as an idea, and who has been, and will be, treated by the South as an idea. *That election was an act of war upon Slavery, — all the more formidable because constitutional.*

It is only in crystals that one sees plainly any mingled substance which is inferior. You cannot see a speck of dirt in the heart of a pebble, but you can see it clearly in the heart of a pure crystal. It is so with the evil at the heart of this country. The wrongs which for ages lay unobserved in the stony heart of absolutism, preserved now in the centre of a republic, discolor all the rays shining through it. Our faith and courage in these times will be in proportion to our realization of the fact that our trouble, though it should end in failure, is a sign not of weakness so much as of strength. Were the age meaner, its claim would not be, as it is now, beyond the ordinary satisfaction of circumstances. Had the evils which afflict us a tongue, it would say: " Surely you have grown very sophisticated and fastidious. Read your school histories over again, and see what age was exempt from injustice and violence, war and Slavery. Are you not making in this generation a great deal of noise over evils that your ancestors sat very quietly under ? " Certainly we are. We stand upon our vantage as proudly as did the young Goethe, of whom it is related that, when six years old, he plagued his mother with questions as to whether the stars would perform for him all that, according to some fortune-teller, they had promised at his birth. " Why," said his mother, " must you have the assistance of the stars, when other people get on very well without ? " To this the terrible child replied : " But I am not to be satisfied with what does for other people." So the humblest man in Christendom to-day puts his foot upon such a government as Jesus and Paul rested quietly under ; so the poorest American is too high to be satisfied with what suits an Austrian. Centuries of rain and sunshine are not wasted on the vineyard of God, where nations of men climb to clusters. Therefore, although the country was never so disturbed before in its immediate interests, it was never higher than now. This sundering of a great Confederacy,—this panic fallen upon all our material interests,— this division of the large church bodies,—all testify gloriously how large a price a young nation is willing to pay for a principle. Never more fitly could it be called a chosen people of God than now, when it says, " Yes, we are ready to press out even into a forty-years wilderness, following the guiding pillar of Liberty, whether it turn to us its fiery or its clouded side ! "

The cannon's roar to-day, then, proclaims Liberty radiant in the heavens. America is assailed only because she has turned from Slavery, and pressed forward to touch the vesture's hem of Freedom. That was her only crime. Then let the prophets be stoned ; let those who proclaim that the axe must and shall be laid to the root of the tree be slain, and the head of Radicalism be brought on a charger to the Herodias of Democracy ! When the Voice in the Wilderness is hushed, the Voice in Jerusalem breaks out.

Here, then, in our Dial of Growths, is the first hour traced, — the nightshade of a fatal and ignoble peace in the midst of crime closes. Far nobler this blood-red flower of war !

Again, I see fast closing beneath the glow that old atheism which has fancied that this world was not governed by the laws of God. It was said by Mr. Gladstone, that "the king of Sicily had reduced atheism to a system of government." That king might certainly, at any time in the last twenty years, have sued the United States government for an infraction of his patent.

And the government was so because the people were so. Would a people ever dream of disregarding habitually laws in which they had faith as involving interests of life and death? Would they eat poisons, launch ships without compasses, leap over precipices? That is just what we have been doing in the real world, — the world where gravitation takes the form of justice. And now comes the severe experience which shows us that the Golden Rule is not only a moral but a physical law; that these invisible laws which are called moral are not abstractions, the violations of which are to end in a grand scenic display of Zamiel with red lights in the future world, but laws which encircle the world above and below, and govern it infallibly in every instant; and that no wrong is without its penalty on the moment. Our nation's crime is to-day its own retribution; the stain on our flag has become a plague-spot on the body. And upon those in our land who most abetted the wrong the retribution is heaviest.

There were sundry atheistic institutions in our land, calling themselves Tract and Missionary Societies: these,

simply for lucre and worldly strength, refused to listen
to the cries or sobs of four millions of their brethren, —
consented that they should be sold into Egypt. Now
come the great hails which sweep away the refuges of
lies; and these very societies and churches which most
failed to rescue those torn and bleeding sheep of Christ's
fold, are the most sundered and ruined. They laid up
their treasures where Confederates break through and
steal. The most flourishing societies and churches now
are those which rebuked slavery too sternly to have
any possessions in the South to be lost.

Trade has also learned its lesson. We had, in the
times of Henry Clay, memorials circulated through
the North, praying Congress to have the discussion of
Slavery in its halls suppressed. They were signed
principally by merchants with large Southern trade.
In some cities, however, there were found merchants
who would not sign away their independence for Southern custom. These the pro-slavery papers were swift
in parading as the enemies of the South, and they
suffered by the withdrawal of Southern custom. The
South dealt more largely than ever with its "friends."
The others had to reorganize their trade : forced to
plant their business entirely in the North, those firms
are to-day secure ; they have no dreary account of
irrecoverable thousands with Southern dealers. Of all
such customers they were long ago relieved by their
compliant neighbors, now groaning under the seques-
tration of their property in the South.

And we may rest assured that all who have woven into their lives and interests rotten and blood-rusted threads, will now see the tissue torn to tatters under the blasts which attend this judgment-day.

Atheism, then, — the disbelief in the reality of Divine laws, — can never again rule in church and trade: they will believe, though for a while it will be only to "believe and tremble."

Let us hope also that the day has advanced enough to close up that old poisonous blossom *Compromise*, and that the new hour is opening *Truth*. Ah, how have we needed the snow-white petals of this flower, in place of that compliant trailing weed!

A lion on a plain was taunted by a serpent, which was on a high, steep rock, with his inability to climb to an equal height. The lion answered, "I might like you have risen, if like you I had crawled." What was all this prosperity, this wealth, this spread-eagle nationality; the first untainted breath sent through the Capitol showed that it was all a crawling prosperity. And so, thank God, the heel of our manhood is near the head of that serpent whose trail was through church and 'change and court and government.

In establishing the government, our fathers compromised; to-day we reap the harvest of that seed; and to-day the people are reading the law, that those who begin with the compromise of principle have given themselves to the toils of a glittering, bright-eyed, golden-scaled serpent, which must inevitably crush them at last. See before you, Americans, the consequences of a compromise proposed and accepted!

Now let us turn into the past, and consider an instance of another kind; an instance of a compromise proposed and rejected, and the consequences of the same. Here is the *compromise proposed:* —

"The Devil taketh him into an exceeding high mountain, and showeth him all the kingdoms of the world and the glory of them; and saith unto him, All these things will I give thee, if thou wilt fall down and worship me."

And here is the *compromise rejected:* —

"Then said Jesus, Get thee behind me, Satan."

And, finally, here are the *consequences:* —

"Then the Devil leaveth him, and, behold, angels came and ministered unto him."

May we not even call this the Messiah of nations, as it stands out in the wilderness, hungry as ever for wealth and plenty, but obeying the spirit which leads it to the trial of its faith in justice and liberty?

This is no metaphor; it is a momentous reality. America is to-day in the wilderness of temptation, and beside her is the Tempter.

Up into the mountain the Tempter leads, — the exceeding high mountain of our national greatness and pride. From that apex, ready to crumble under our feet, how keenly the kingdoms of this world and their glories strike the senses! On one side, the kingdom of political unity; on another, the kingdom of cotton; near by, the realms of trade; and there, the kingdom of ecclesiastical power. The Tempter never slumbers so long as God is awake. " What is it," he whispers, " that divides your nation? what is it that prevents cotton from crystallizing to diamonds for your treasury? what is it that hangs the auction-flag from the windows of trade? what is it that sunders every church? It is your hatred of African Slavery. It is your love of freedom. Only give over these, — only consent to the fetter on the limbs of the black man, — and see, all these kingdoms are yours, with all their glories! See, the nation is one again; the coffer is full. The Church's wounds are healed so soon as Northern and Southern Christians consent to kneel around a common altar, there to eat the broken body and drink the shed blood of the African race. All these shall be yours, says the Tempter, if only ye will turn from the shrine of Liberty, and worship Slavery; and you may call your idol patriotism, union, concession, compromise, fraternal feeling, peace, or any other fine name you please."

Never before was the Compromise-devil foiled in this country. Let that be forever named " an exceeding high mountain," where the people confront the Tempter without kneeling, where not one man dear to the people is heard saying, This be thy god, O America!

But, side by side, there are yet growing two blood-stained growths, with petals full blown; they are Slavery and War: near them two fair white buds, whose names are Liberty and Peace. Comrades, faint not, but watch and labor and wait, that those flame-leaved, sickening blossoms may close, as they must, *together;* and in that moment unfolding, these snowy, healing ones shall record that it is Freedom's noontide.

XVIII.

THE GOLDEN HOUR.

THERE is an Oriental legend which relates that a poor man sat a thousand years before the gates of Paradise; then, in his weariness, he snatched one hour's sleep. But in that hour the gates of pearl swung open, and the poor man awoke just in time to see them close.

Long has this country been sitting in dust and rags before the barred gates of Liberation from the curse which is upon her. In our midst reigned the infernal institution which seemed to preserve the deadliest blood-drops of all the tyrants the world ever saw. It crushed all heart and hope out of the black man; it laid waste his home, and made the earth for him a great devil's masterpiece; but it could not so wrong him as it has wronged the white man. From the white man it took the very marrow of honor. It has made it a life-long battle to be a gentleman in this country, Slavery insisting that one shall be a coward and a Negro-hound. O God! to see our President's own State wallowing in the very sewers of Slavery with its black laws, until one longs for some Toussaint to scourge Illinois of black hearts, and fill it with black faces! To see Ohio, ruled by the vermin who tremble to take a Confederate officer's slave or sword in her own capital, stoning any man of common sense and common honesty who would have her go a step beyond pork and whiskey! To see this institution, after treading under its feet the millions of black bodies and the souls of whites in the South, marching on through the North, its brass collar on the necks of five Representatives of Massachusetts, — a Republican Cabinet afraid to look it in the eye! Alas! it is not four, but nearer twenty-four, millions of slaves we have in America.

But now has the Golden Hour come, and with a song from every angel, a shriek from every demon, the pearly portals of Liberation are prized open by Slavery's own madness, and America is invited to enter the blessed land.

Last year Republicans had to be technical and skilful in proving even a probability that at the bottom of the ballot-box a gateway of release would ever be found; to-day it requires all the ingenuity of the Cabinet engineers *not* to free us. Their great problem now is, how not to do it.

How long have the opponents of this nation's crime been met with the complaint that they were trying to hurry God? "Cannot you let Providence do its own work?" "Providence will do away with the evil in its own good time."

To all of which, not without a suspicion of its hypocrisy, the antislavery man could only reply, with Luther, " God is a good worker, but loves to be helped."

But now, if ever " providential hour " and " God's own good time " meant anything, they are here. The hour has arrived when Slavery comes outside of constitutional and legal intrenchments, and makes its death the alternative of the death of the nation. The hour has come when the lives of our best and bravest, and the bread of the poor, are dependent on its overthrow. The hour has come when for the first time we have an army gathered sufficient in numbers and appointments to secure us infallibly against those fancied dangers which have been held up to affright the timid, as following in the train of emancipation.

But where are all our Providentialists? Where are those who bade us await God's own good time? O ye resigned ones, who so piously suppressed your enthusiasm for freedom lest you should upset God's plans, do not all speak at once!

How does God's " own good time " passing over our heads find us? Behold, the Bridegroom cometh. At the altar of Justice, Liberty would wed America. Where are the lamps, filled, trimmed, and ready?

Foolish virgins, whilst ye go to buy, the door shall be shut! What avails all our toiling, suffering, pleading, — what avails the reddened soil of Kansas, what the blood of the martyrs, — if now the golden portal of opportunity to which these have brought us shall be shut in our faces?

An old journal had this singular advertisement in the column of " Losses " : —

" LOST. — *Yesterday, somewhere between sunrise and sunset, a Golden Hour, set with sixty diamond minutes.*"

No reward was offered, doubtless because the loser knew that the priceless jewel was gone forever.

Golden is every hour ; but there are periods when moments are hours, and hours years, and years ages. Who can appraise the hours which arrive, one by one, Sibyl-like, each proffering the sacred volumes in which the victorious destiny of a Free Republic is written ? Who can hear the full mournfulness of the word " Lost," but they who know that, as each hour departs, it goes to burn another of those volumes ? Meanwhile, the steadfast oracle proclaims that, when the last hour which gives us the opportunity of emancipation passes, the doom of this Union is sealed.

Not one hour passes over this nation, but in it — in that one hour — the nightmare of ages might be hurled from its breast. This hour a decree that henceforth the United States ignores utterly the relation of master and slave paralyzes, as by the voice of a god, every arm uplifted against the country, and, which is far better, saves it from its own blindness here on the precipice's verge. The Sibyl, Opportunity, has not yet left the slave forever; his eyes strain toward the hope which has not yet set; anon he has sent up his signals of flame to see if the army of the North is his friend or enemy. But the slave knows, and we know, that his status in this struggle must soon be settled; nay, in some points it is already settled, and he stands the armed foe of the United States. As soon as it is determined that this is not *his* Golden Hour, he chooses between two foes; and why should he not choose the side of those who represent the evil he knows, over those representative of the evils he knows not of? Why should he fly to those who esteem his rights beneath the rights of traitors, thieves, and assassins? Why should he select those who can do him no harm where he is, in preference to those who may still hold power over his wife and child and parent?

The Golden Hour will not wait on us to the measure of our own moral cowardice. " We should not be in haste to determine that radical measures are necessary," says the President. True, but we should be as much without rest as without haste, for no hour will bear to have its task put off upon another hour. The present hour offers us a peaceful victory through emancipation. The next may offer us only

victory by that means. The third may offer us a
costly victory, provided we can provide arms for the
slaves. The fourth may make it as difficult to do
this, as it is now to furnish arms to the loyal men
of East Tennessee. The fifth may sweep away our
advantages altogether, and our Golden Hour, crossed
by a scythe, become a symbol on our nation's grave.

Our President and legislators talk of this advantage — our only advantage, mark — of using liberty
to save the country, as if Time was in their pay.
Time is in the pay of those who take him by the
forelock : he is all bald behind.

When the commanding general at Washington announced that every soldier found guilty of sleeping
on duty should be shot, some of us were alarmed
by an apprehension that he would have to begin at
the head of the army, and shoot all, down to the
drummer-boy. So far as the country knew, the whole
army of the Potomac was fast asleep.

There is in history no other instance of an army
within sight of an enemy sleeping away seasons so
fair. Why was that strange hesitancy? " The army
must be re-organized " : we waited until it had
passed its maximum of organization, and began to
decline. " The rivers are too highly swollen " : we
stood still until they had subsided. " The roads are
utterly impassable for artillery " : we waited until
they were dry. " When the leaves fall " : the last

leaf fell. "An attack from the enemy is momentarily expected ": we waited, and it came not. "Secretary Deepdiver remarked to-day, in conversation with a gentleman, that the country would be gratified by stirring news in ten days ": twenty pass, and not a stir.

The nation arraigned this slumber of their military energies, and has awaited the plea of its commanders. Thoughtless nation, your commanders had a very sufficient plea. They slept because the nation slept. Their eyes were heavy because atmospheric conditions cannot be resisted. A certain black drug, infused into the atmosphere of this country, has made open eyes sectional, and Sleepy Hollow national; and, as Rip Van Winkle shouted for King George before the astonished subjects of the United States, the graduates of a certain institution, undoubtedly built on the verge of Sleepy Hollow, have not yet heard that we are no longer colonies of the South, and subjects of Slavery.

General McClellan occupied his position at the head of the United States forces, not because he had lived or served up to that position, — for several silly proclamations in Western Virginia, the Potomac blockade, and Ball's Bluff were all on his record, and not one great deed, — but simply because, when his superiors snored, he was not so disrespectful as to keep awake. He is not a large man, neither is he a fool; and he could peep through his eyelids enough to see what befell such wakeful spirits as Fremont and Lane. General McClellan was not and is not a traitor ; but in this war every pro-slavery heart is, whether consciously or not, a partially disloyal heart, because it cannot possibly be awake to the real forces in this conflict. It was fixed in his mind that no person who should slay many Southerners could fail to exasperate the South, and both sections would never unite sweetly upon any such man.

It would have been impossible for McClellan to have remained commander during that long inaction, if the people had not been in a rusty, sleepy transition state : when they first sat up in bed, they called for some such man as Stanton ; for the President is the faithful tongue of the people's *wishes*, however poorly he may supply their *wants*.

Well, in a military sense we have waked up ; but in dealing intelligently and directly with the cause and support of the Rebellion we are repeating the McClellan slumber over again. In this higher army than the military, it would be a formidable order to have all the sentinels who sleep at their posts shot.

There is our honored President, for example, none can doubt that he is wide awake before the portal of Military Opportunity ; but before the open door by which our nation may pass onward to liberation from all that makes war possible, he gives scarcely a sign. It is evident that the worthy President would *like to* have God on his side : he *must* have Kentucky.

In all this the nation hears only the echo of its own loud snore. What are leaders to do when, at a time when the very existence of the nation is threatened, they hear sensible men asking old cant questions about the Negroes, and what to do with them?

Is the Negro descended from the same original pair with the Caucasian? — For what is the use of our nation's being saved, if it is not ethnologically saved?

Will not the Negro steal our silver spoons? How dreary were a spoonless nationality! (A happy thought! We can employ Floyd or some other Caucasian as a missionary to inculcate honesty to Negroes.)

What is meant in the Scriptures by "Cursed be Canaan"? For, of course, national existence is nothing if not exegetical?

Again, what is the origin of evil? For is not death better than unteleological life?

That we should be spending three millions a day, and our men perishing by thousands, whilst we discuss the destiny and capacity of the negro, reminds one of the position taken by Anacharsis Clootz in the French Assembly, "that the democratic principle was of such importance, that it would be cheaply purchased by the total destruction of the human race from the face of the planet"!

What shall be done with the Negro, forsooth! Can we do any worse with him than we have done, and are doing? Can he be any heavier burden to us than now, when he is the fulcrum on which turns every lever set to overthrow our liberties and lives? May we not respectfully submit that it is about as much as we can attend to, to take care of Society in 1862, without adjusting the social relations and conditions of 1962? May it not be surmised that the future will have brains to attend to its own affairs? May we not suggest, also, that, having once decided what we would " do with the Negro," Almighty God does n't seem to have been over pleased at our disposal of him in that instance, and seems very likely to have a share in any future disposal of him?

Accuse not thy generals, O American nation! Thou art the drugged sleeper. Before thee with thy heavy-eyed millions, Liberty, in sight of the swords and staves of avowed foes and seeming friends, which threaten its life, stands appealing, " Couldst thou not watch with me one hour? " It may be that Liberty shall have to say presently to the slumbering sentinels, " Sleep on now: my hour is come " ; — and must needs pass to its resurrection through the dark portal of her chosen nation's grave.

XIX.

THE NEGRO.

MONTESQUIEU said that it would not do to suppose that Negroes were men, lest it should turn out that whites were not.

The sarcasm falls almost exclusively upon this country, where alone the indecent nonsense concerning the nature of the Negro survives. In 1781, in the case of the ship Zong, whose master had thrown one hundred and thirty-two slaves alive into the sea to cheat the underwriters, the first jury gave a verdict in favor of the master and owners: they had a right to do what they had done. Lord Mansfield is reported to have said on the bench: " The matter left to the jury is, Was it from necessity? For they had no doubt — though it shocks one very much — that the case of slaves was the same as if horses had been thrown overboard." Such was the Negro in the eye of the law when Sharpe and Clarkson began their efforts. The latter of these, early in his career, made a collection of African productions and manufactures, as indications of what the Negro, despite all disparagements, had attained. They were considered remarkable by some of the best judges in England. Mr. Pitt was especially interested in them. " On sight of these," says Clarkson, " many sublime thoughts seemed to rush at once into his mind, some of which he expressed." From this time the project, which was always dear to him, of the civilization of Africa arose in his mind. A half-century of healthy development brought England to its senses as regards the Negro.

Since then the Negro has lived to prove that those who are counting upon perpetual degradation and final extermination as his destiny are running against the grain of things. He has shown a vitality equal to that of the white race, where both are out of their native climates; and where the white man has been vindicating his claim to superiority only by enslaving him, — empowered to do so by having armed nations behind him, — the Negro has shown himself easily superior to his master. This he has always proved as soon as the outside pressure of law and force was removed, and a fair trial of strength between him and his master permitted. He has become the dominant race in the West Indies; he has superseded the white man in Haïti altogether; and the unanimous verdict of our soldiers now in the South is, that the Negro is the superior race in that section of America. Of the eight millions of whites in the Slave States, six are "poor white trash," and no one who has seen them can compare them to the black laborers there. And when it comes to upper classes, it is not easy to decide that Jeff Davis's coachman is better fitted to be the slave than the master of Jeff, or that Robert Small is not equal to Pickens, Floyd, or any of their set.

At Monticello the exquisite mosaic floor, made by one of Mr. Jefferson's slaves, is yet in good preservation. The old friend of that statesman who showed it to me said: "Mr. Jefferson always took pleasure in showing his visitors this exquisite piece of workmanship. It was made by one of his slaves, born on his estate, who never had any instruction as a mechanic. Mr. Jefferson always believed that the Negro race had a destiny."

There is the important fact; there lies the Enceladus under this volcano, — THE NEGRO HAS AN IMPORTANT DESTINY TO FULFIL IN HUMAN SOCIETY. Our laws and plans have been arranged with reference to another theory: we had assumed his moral and political non-existence, and in so doing we have gone, day by day, more and more against the eternal fact. And unless we speedily have that lie which this nation has actively credited purged out of it, it will drag us into the abyss prepared for lies from before the foundation of the world. Elwood Fisher has prepared for this nation an epitaph which runs: "Here lies a people who lost their own liberty in trying to give freedom to the Negro." The hope is too high for us to indulge, that this nation can thus become the dying Saviour among the nations! If the nation should perish, history would engrave on its tomb, "Here lies a people who lost their own liberty in trying to pursue through a Red Sea those for whose liberty God had parted the waves."

The worst symptom in the case of America is the prejudice against the Negro, — a disease which always has called for fearful cauterization. What is in refined society unmitigated vulgarity, is in this country considered elegance. A few years ago, President Roberts of Liberia was returning from America through England. The captain of the steamship would not allow this cultivated and distinguished gentleman to sit at table with the white passengers; and persisted in his refusal, even after a majority of the whites had requested otherwise. A day after their arrival in England, Mr. Roberts, having some business with the captain, repaired to the steamship, and found him in the presence of many of the passengers who had witnessed his treatment on board. On being addressed, the captain said to President Roberts, " Come down this evening at 8 o'clock, and I will attend to you." " At that hour," replied Roberts, " I am engaged to dine with the Queen of England." The confused captain named another hour, amidst the explosive laughter of the company. This Negro, so offensive to the steamboat aristocracy of America, is received as diplomatic minister in every other government of Christendom, and at Rome the African bishop stands beside the whitest who in America may be helping to enslave his race. Is there wonder that in many parts of Europe "American" should be synonymous with "vulgar"?

It has been whispered that Haïti will appoint a white

man to act for that country at Washington. I cannot believe that the President of Haïti could so far degrade his country before the world as to make such an appointment; but if there are any such influences at work, it behooves every friend of freedom to protest loudly and strongly against it. If Haïti cannot be represented here by her blackest Negro, let her be unrepresented; this nation already perceives that we need her more than she needs us. But more than all the fruits, spices, and wealth she can bring us, we need her black minister in Washington. We need him there as the touchstone of our civilization; we need him as the magic mantle to reveal every sham and every impurity in the Republican Court.

"I esteem," says Emerson, "the occasion of this jubilee (West Indian Emancipation) to be the proud discovery that the black race can contend with the white; that, in the great anthem which we call History, a piece of many parts and vast compass, after playing a long time a very low and subdued accompaniment, they perceive the time arrived when they can strike in with effect, and take a master's part in the music. The civility of the world has reached that pitch, that their more moral genius is becoming indispensable, and the quality of this race is to be honored for itself. For this they have been preserved in sandy deserts, in rice swamps, in kitchens and shoe-shops, so long; now let them emerge, clothed and in their own form."

No danger from the Southern Confederacy threatens us so much as this cry of our rulers for the colonization of freed Negroes. A million square miles of untilled lands to which their sinews are by the laws of Nature consecrated, are clamoring for them, and yet madmen in power are talking of exiling them! Haïti, Liberia, and now the Danish government, are all intriguing to get these laborers from us; and nothing but the resolution of the Negroes, that they will not go unless forced, saves us from this fearful loss. America will one day kneel, and thank that people that they held out against the stupidity and ignorance of the colonizationists, whose projects would blight one half of our territory. If, by any unfortunate means, America shall be robbed of this race, posterity will know the President under whom the exodus occurs only by the name of FOOL.

What are we to do with the Negro? Is the Anglo-Saxon brain on this hemisphere softening? If so, some day in the midst of wasted fields and desolate lands, we may be burdened with the question, What can we do without him?

No! this race is to remain with us; it has brought from the remote past and fervid East a sacred stream of vitality, by it alone now represented upon earth, which it is appointed to mingle with the current of humanity, and without which man in the New World could never fill out the outlines sketched for him by the Supreme Artist.

X X.

TO THE PRESIDENT OF THE UNITED STATES.

HONORED SIR : — Passing homeward one night, about three years ago, I encountered a large crowd, who were listening to some speaker. A crowd in the market space of our Queen City was nothing unusual, and I was thinking only how to open my way through it, when, in clear, earnest tones, these words fell upon my ear : " I am satisfied that the only just and effectual method of dealing with Slavery is that which shall always recognize and deal with it AS WRONG."

In a moment I turned, and remained for over an hour to hear a powerful statement of which that sentence was the key-note. The next time I saw that speaker it was as he passed along the same street, amid the ovations of the people who had helped to elect him as a President who should deal with Slavery as a great wrong, — how great they did not then know, or much more than surmise.

Since that day, Sir, in which the sight of a duly-elected honest, antislavery President filled our eyes with happy tears, this country has seen nothing which does not indicate that you *mean* to deal with the accursed thing *as wrong.*

Though your administration had been proved to have exhausted itself in having called out seventy-five thousand men to defend the integrity of this nation, the people could never have forgotten that, in doing so, you did a greater deed than Cortez, burning the ships of ignoble compromise behind us.

But, Sir, your administration did not exhaust itself in that: the laurels shall never fade which twine about the brow of the President under whose administration Slavery was abolished in the District, and Haïti recognized, and Emancipation first proposed from the White House.

But all these things will not save this Republic from dissolution. No one who has ever looked of late into your eye, as I have, can fail to see that every fibre of heart and brain in you has become identified with the rescue of this Union from the perils which threaten it, and that there is no personal sacrifice which you could not make for that end. Nor can any observing person fail to see that the tendency of your mind and action is steadily toward Emancipation; whilst many, who know that in such an emergency as this a day is often a century, feel keenly that, not for the slave's sake, but for our own, we need sharp, bold, decisive, in a word, *heroic* action.

The naturalist Thoreau used to amuse us much by thrusting his hand into the Concord River, and drawing out at will a fine fish, which would lie quietly in his hand: when we thrust in ours, the fish would scamper out of reach. It seemed like a miracle, until he explained to us that his power to take up the fish depended upon his knowledge of the color and location of the fish's eggs. The fish will protect its spawn; and when Thoreau placed his hand underneath that, the fish, in order to protect it, would swim immediately over it, and the fingers had only to close for it to be caught.

Slavery is the spawn out of which the armed forces of treason and rebellion in the South have been hatched; and by an inviolable instinct they will rush, at any cost, to protect Slavery. You have only, Sir, to take Slavery in your grasp, then close your fingers around the rebellion.

This I have tried to prove; also, that the only way of grasping the rebellion-spawn is to declare that this nation no longer recognizes the institution of Slavery as in existence. This we humbly implore you to do, by the martial power which Slavery has compelled you to use in place of the normal powers of the Constitution. For, Sir, from the day in which Slavery became to this government an outlaw, Liberty became, like ancient Thebes, hundred-gated.

It is a high circumstance, Sir, whether its full bearing was seen by our fathers or not, that the commander-in-chief of our army and navy is at the same time the .chief guardian of our national honor and political liberties; and whilst a mere military general may have no higher draft to make upon martial power than that which will enable him to make this

or that expedition successful, we have a right to claim
that our President shall raise a higher standard of
Necessity, — one including not only the preservation
of our national existence, but of that security without military despotism, that honor without stain, which
alone can make existence worthy of preservation.

The air is full of noisy objections against the request of your petitioners for an edict of emancipation.
Some of these remind me of the Sheik's objection to
lending his rope.   When Abul Alladin asked of him
the loan of a rope, the Sheik said, "I need it to tie
up a measure of sand."   "Need a rope to tie up
sand!" exclaimed Abul in astonishment.   "O neighbor," replied the Sheik, "any reason will do when
one does not wish to lend a thing."   There is no use
in dealing with objections which arise from the desire
and determination to retain Slavery in this country,
at any time; certainly none in addressing one who
has declared his determination to recognize and deal
with it only as wrong.

The people have witnessed with indignation how
those who lately denounced you as a sectional candidate, because they saw that, if you reached the White
House, *you* would be the President, and not Slavery,
are now at Washington, standing in the shoes yet
warm from the feet of traitors, and, in the interest
of Slavery, throwing it perpetually in your face that
you entered the arena upon the platform of non-inter-
ference with Slavery in the States.   You, Sir, cannot

be deceived by such twaddle; and if you fear that any honest people are, I pray you to dismiss the misgiving. They know, Sir, that interference with Slavery in the States was not in your Chicago Platform; they know also that the loss of twenty thousand men pursuant to your proclamation was not in your Chicago Platform. The remedy must change with the disease: the physician may give an appropriate medicine for measles; but if the measles should presently change to small-pox, what should we say of a physician who ⸺hould attempt to vindicate his consistency by giving the same medicine after the disease had changed? The Chicago Platform prescribed for measles; but you have to treat a virulent case of small-pox, and the patient will not last until you can get party-men to make a new platform.

It is demonstrable, Sir, that in every point of view — constitutional, ethical, or personal — you have more right to kill an institution that injures man, than you have to kill a man. Institutions at the best are the mere scaffoldings about man.

But you are assured that this measure would divide the North. In contradiction of this, we have the lesson of a recent experience. One of our generals did, in the face of the world, take the God of Justice on his side; he who had planted our banner on the highest point of land in America found a higher height, and planted it there, when he declared every slave free whom he could declare free. What was the result?

Like a crystal stream from everlasting hills upon a parched and thirsty land came his proclamation ; the nation was filled with joy and power ; the young men sprang to their feet as they read it, and their hearts throbbed with a divine enthusiasm ; rank after rank poured westward, and Europe for the first and only time glowed with sympathy and admiration. Even the vilest presses which had been dragged along after our banner — the New York *Herald,* the Boston *Courier* and *Post,* and Cincinnati *Enquirer* — seemed to feel a touch of nobleness, and cried Bravo! to the Pathfinder as he scaled this loftier height than any sierra. All felt that it was our only great victory, our compensation for every defeat. For one noble week we were a united, electrified, invincible nation. Alas! since that week a humiliated, discontented, divided, muttering nation, we have been but a monument of the tremendous power of that invisible thing called Justice, to uplift those who ally themselves therewith, and to divide and weaken those who " modify " her plain mandates. From that week we have been divided, and the only token of a return to the same unity appeared when our President took lately a step toward that standard of liberty which he had furled for reasons which seemed to him patriotic and necessary. And as he shall take step after step upward and onward, more and more will he find the North gather into a solid phalanx around him.

" But our officers and soldiers would lay down their arms." As far as our soldiers are concerned, this is but a base and silly libel. The records show that enlistments tripled in number after Fremont's proclamation, all the soldiers wishing to go into his department; and that they were seriously checked when that edict of freedom was modified. As for our generals, it would be one of the best things about such an edict that it *might* cause some of them to resign ; — I hope the majority would go home, with their friends Patterson and Stone, who have gone before. Who would not be glad to hear that every half-hearted leader had been cowed back by the determined front of Liberty, which he had pretended to serve whilst really serving Slavery ? Once, says an old fable, the cat, hearing that the hen was sick, went to pay her a visit. After condoling with the invalid, the cat said, " Really, I should like to serve you in any way in my power. What can I do for you ? " The invalid hen cast an uneasy glance at the yellow eyes and hungry chops of the cat, and replied, " You can do me a signal service by leaving me. I think if you will leave me, I shall be much better." Some people's room is better than their company; and amongst these may be reckoned those who, in a war for Liberty, esteem it their duty to hunt down, to crush with an iron hand, to refuse entrance within their lines to the innocent and wronged who seek *their* liberty also ; or who know so little of the old Orphic strain to which the walls of the universe arose, as to drive from their camp the minstrels who sing of LIBERTY.

With reference, however, to this fear of dividing the North or their army, we may admit that the kindling and spreading of such a fire would rouse up some nests of serpents in both. But those who have studied most deeply epochs related to that through which we are now passing, know how fatal has been any waiting for complete unity.

No cause has ever kindled the enthusiasm which could sustain it to the end, until it was elevated enough to slough off its baser adherents.

No cause ever produced the heroes necessary to its real and final victory, until it was pure enough to separate, as on God's threshing-floor, the chaff from the wheat.

Our fathers of the Revolution never gained any great victories until the war about taxes became a war for complete independence ; but when that period came, they had to fight the Tories with one hand and the British with the other. For a long time it was difficult to say whether Tories or Independents were in the majority ; but the world was given again to see that strength does not lie in majorities, but rather in causes so glorious that every man standing for them is a hundred-fold the man he would be fighting on the lowest plane.

As for more division coming of the elevation of our cause than is implied in this weeding and winnowing of our ranks, a higher force enters in all such cases to prevent it. That higher force is HEROISM. *That* electric battery has a line to every human heart.

The demagogues do not estimate this in making their calculations. We had a little over a year ago Governors of Free States declaring that any troops marching southward must fight their militia first. We had a Senator declaring that disunion would run a ploughshare along the great National Road. Mr. Lincoln resolved that he would stand or fall by the Republic, and answered all these prophecies with the call for an army, and lo! instead of a ploughshare dividing the Northwest, instead of a fire in the rear, the North, which Daniel Webster said had no existence, rises as one man at his heroic call. The first touch of heroism in the government created anew this nation.

Then the demagogues said, "But just touch a slave, and these men will lay down their arms." Fremont, as we have seen, responds with a declaration that the slaves of rebels are freemen, and the country gathers about him with a tenacity which jealous officials and investigating committees strive vainly to weaken.

If there is anything proved by our experience in this war, it is that one true man may chase ten thousand old-line Democrats. Try it, Mr. President; remember that your boldest word has had the noblest echo from the people, and try a braver one yet! Utter, loud enough for the nation, the slave, the world to hear, the watchword, LIBERTY TO ALL, and though traitors in the North may writhe, they shall be as fangless as the Rebellion shall thenceforth be; for every true heart upon this earth is at your side from that instant, to live and to die.

You will hear the cry "Abolitionist!" no doubt: I will not believe that it can terrify you. What is an Abolitionist? He is simply a man who desires liberty for the entire family of man: — this is a wretch dastardly enough to oppose having that done to another man, his wife and child, which he would not like to have done to himself, his wife and child! George Washington, when he declared that the first wish of his heart was to have Slavery abolished, — George Washington, when he called to be Chief Justice of the United States the founder and President of the New York Abolition Society, John Jay, — was this monster, an Abolitionist! His real farewell address, the will made on his death-bed, freeing his slaves, was an appeal for abolition.

I believe there are few who doubt that it is your jealous care for the interests of the Border States, and a (supposed) large number of Unionists in the far South, that constitutes the chief obstacle in the way of this radical cure. Even so far as their own testimony on this subject is concerned, we have no reason to believe that the real Southern Unionists are represented in this emergency by the men who have been sent to Washington merely by habit in comparatively unimportant times. What reason have we to believe that Southern Unionists are represented by Andy Johnson or Mr. Crittenden, more than Ohioans by Vallandingham? The people do not reach you so skilfully or readily as these politicians. I remember, Sir, to have heard you expressing a doubt as to the readiness of these people for any dealing with Slavery, when a moment before I had been conversing with a very intelligent Unionist from Florida, a large proprietor and slaveholder in that State, who informed me that he had been in the anteroom of the White House for several hours a day for nearly three weeks, without being received or heard. He came to give it as his opinion, and that of the half-dozen Union men whom he knew in his State, that to abolish Slavery was the one way of putting down the Rebellion. I fear that many of those hours were occupied by men from the Border States who would not have represented the real loyalists of the South half so well. An acquaintance of some years with the people of the mountain ranges extending through Maryland down to Alabama leads me to affirm that two thirds of them would welcome a decree of emancipation by the government; whilst a generous response would not fail from the eighteen thousand Germans of New Orleans, and the five thousand apiece of Richmond and Louisville. Of Missouri I need not speak: nothing but a disability in the Constitution of that State prevents an almost immediate response to your offer of " co-operation." That State had, before the Rebellion broke out, 150,000 slaves; it now has less than 50,000. A decree of emancipation, paying loyal masters of course, would be a great relief to that State from its complications.

There is but a very small number of loyal slaveholders in the Border States; and surely they could not show their loyalty more than by refusing to allow this slight interest to stand in the way of the national safety. What would the country say, if, when you asked men owning land around Washington or St. Louis to yield their land and houses, that national defences might be made perfect, they had refused ? They would be esteemed disloyal, and their lands taken. You, sir, have given the handful of slaveholders in the Border States a good military reason why they should emancipate, in your special message ; to the country it seems a sufficient touchstone of their loyalty or disloyalty.

Suppose they should not receive the full market value for their slaves, — though we could pay that at far less cost than allow them to remain slaves, — should the loyalists of the Slave States have more indemnity than the loyalists of the Free States ? Are we not all, on account of this institution they are hugging, losing our business, income, paying enormous taxes? Shall our capitalists in the Free States demand of the government so much on the dollar for all they have lost ? Loyal men, North and South, must expect to lose ; and though to hush the crying children, and to be generous to those who are unused to labor, we are all willing to compensate these Southern loyalists, yet in strict justice the injured commerce of the North has as much right to demand compensation.

In God's name, let us have no half-work in this

matter! This pitiful little interest must not spancel the nation in the great stride now demanded of it. Though to them emancipation itself will bring wealth and more lasting benefits, yet let them be paid ; as Sumner said, "A bridge of gold would be cheap, should the retreating fiend demand it."

One stroke of Titian's brush, it is said, changed the face of a leopard to that of a beautiful woman. Freedom is a finer artist, and beneath her touch, barren Virginia and wasted Kentucky and semi-chaotic Missouri would have their myriad sleeping energies break forth into smiling bloom and beauty.

Do you think, Sir, that, after this fearful experience, the American people would welcome you and hail you as their national saviour if you should restore them the Union with Slavery in it ? Never, never! The masses may tell you so, little knowing what a return to the Union with Slavery in it means : but it would not take long to teach them, and they would heap your name with curses!

You may think, and they may think, that it would be a safe experiment to try : you may say, "The institution must be on the down-hill : it can never rule the country again." O, Sir, I beseech you to remember that it was precisely because Slavery seemed to our fathers to be on the down-hill, precisely because they thought they saw its grave already dug in the limitation of the slave-trade, that they suffered it to exist in the new government. They dealt with it as on the down-hill, and lo ! we reap the bitter results of their mistake.

Slavery has far less appearance now of being on the down-hill than it had then.

Good things come hard ; but you have only to leave your field unoccupied by valuable growths one season for it to be filled with weeds. If you could give us the Union again with Slavery in it, — which God forbid ! — it would only be for the old strife of wheat and tare to be renewed, only to have new war-fires kindled in which to burn the tares which the enemy is ever ready to sow and foster.

But, Sir, it is very plain that the alternative of restoring the Union with Slavery in it is not longer before you : you are to restore us the Union without Slavery, or you are to restore to us a country with its form of government radically changed. These are the alternatives. The sword can kill the body, but not the soul : it must leave the disloyal element, the moral causes of rebellion, in full activity. The sword cannot change muttering hate to love, or treachery to good faith. It is fundamental in the theory of our government, that, from the Presidency down to a village justice, people must be represented by officers elected by themselves and from their own midst. There could never have been any obstacle to the glorious development of republican government in this country, had we not taken into it a so-called institution whose nature it was to prey upon the very tissues of all government. That which monarchies had been unable to get along with, we tried to preserve in a republic ; and the experiment has turned out like the ancient ·mode of punishment which bound a living body limb to limb, face to face, with a rotting corpse, until the living should perish by the stench of the dead.

Now, either we must cut the cords which bind us to this body of death, or it must assimilate us to itself; either we must be free from Slavery, or we must adopt its rules, — we must impose masters upon eight millions of people, we must rule by military patrol, we must suspend the guaranties of the citizen's rights for military reasons. And thus American Liberty, from being a rock under our feet, would become the merest shifting quicksand.

Every time, Sir, that the gates of Forts Warren and Lafayette swung open, the shriek of their hinges pierced every heart in America which knew the sacred value of those writs and forms which Treason compelled you to set aside; for they knew that, whilst you could be trusted, it was not certain that your successor could be. Our fathers had a good old version of a Psalm which ran thus : —

> " He digged a pit,
> He digged it deep,
> He digged it for his brother,
> But through his sin,
> He did fall in
> The pit he digged for t' other."

Would it not be poetic justice, Mr. President, if, Slav-

ery having digged this pit of arbitrary and martial law
for us, it should be allowed to slide into the pit it
" digged for t' other"?

Sir, in five years the most ardent Universalist would
provide a special clause for the everlasting damnation
of the man who helps to have that pit filled up without
Slavery being at the bottom of it!

Let me not be regarded as one of those who are
ready to cavil at the President's use of these unusual
powers; they were used honestly, firmly, and in no case
for persecution; but there were many who could not
help thinking how much better it were if the same
ends could be reached by sacrificing, not a pound of
living flesh, but the cancer feeding on that flesh, —
not the writ of *Habeas Corpus*, but the base interest
that makes men traitors!

The Hour I have called Golden, but it comes to
us in sombre, dreary habiliments. Ah, God! to pass
through these hospitals where lie the young men who
a year ago were the ruddy flowers of happy homes!
To see the wounded, rebel and loyal, seated on straw
in wagons, foot-sole to foot-sole, the same clear, frank
eyes meeting each other, the same young, honest
voices from both, and *not* to see the horrid demon
driving both! Alas for the hearts on the battle-field
and those at home; for the ball that pierces any soldier's heart never lodges there, but speeds onward to
pierce other hearts far away; and for the broken
prophecies and promises of life; for those whose life

ebbs away to-day where no hand is near to soothe, no kind one near to receive the last sigh, and treasure for the dear ones at home the last message of love!

You are our President, and, in a sacred sense, these are all your children; and now you seem to me like one whose name you bear, and who, in obedience to the first Voice which he heard, laid his beloved son upon the altar of the Highest; but when thus his faith was proved, lo, an angel appeared, and cried, Stay thy hand! and the angel pointed to a brute which God had provided for that sacrifice in place of his son. Father, you have done well in obeying the first voice which called for the painful sacrifice of your own children; but listen well, I implore you, if there be not an angel of peace crying, Stay thy hand! Watch well if there be not a shining finger pointing to the BRUTE which, and which alone, God hath provided for the sacrifice of this hour!

XXI.

SURSUM CORDA.

LEADEN is the casket before us, and on it is written, "Who chooseth me must give and hazard all he hath."

Leaden, meagre, and pale; but he is a fool who would choose the caskets of gold and silver in its place; for it contains LIBERTY.

Bresquet, jester to Francis I., kept a Calendar of Fools. When Charles V., confiding in the generosity of Francis, passed through France to appease the rebellion of Gaunt, Bresquet put that Emperor into the Calendar of Fools. His king asked him the cause. He answered, "Because you have suffered at the hands of Charles the greatest bitterness that ever prince did from another; nevertheless, he would trust his person into your hands." "Why, Bresquet," said the king, "what wilt thou say if thou seest him pass back in as great safety as if he marched through the midst of Spain." Said Bresquet, "Why, then I will put him out of the Calendar of Fools, and put you in."

History also keeps a Calendar of Fools.

It has already ascribed it to the insanity and folly, which, thank God, form such large composite parts of all evil, that Slavery has cast off its legal protection, and passes through the country it has so foully wronged, a branded felon and outlaw. But if this be asinine in Slavery, what place in History's Calendar of Fools will be too prominent for this nation, should it permit this devil to pass as safely as ever, crushing under his cloven foot every fair growth of Liberty, and impudently defying the country upon which he has brought every conceivable woe?

There is danger that, if left to our politicians, this golden hour will simply inscribe "Yankee" on the Calendar of Fools; for there is nothing so unfathomably stupid as moral cowardice. "Fear nothing but fear," says Montaigne. To-day you can count on the fingers of one hand the men in Washington who can say *Abolitionist* without the normal prefix *damned*. When the President, even, wishes to use the phrase in a friendly way, he says Abolish*ment*. It is plain that these men can be used by the earnest hearts of America only for filtration. As the waters of our great Western rivers are passed through filters of stone before they are clear enough to drink, so the somewhat muddy streams of American Liberty must find in Cabinet and Congress their stony filters, whose restraint will be purifying.

But it will be purifying only if we see that the streams pass through them: remaining checked by them, the waters shall become stagnant and poisonous.

We have no Joshua to bid the sun stand still and

prolong our Golden Hour beyond its last diamond minute. Meanwhile, the inevitable horizon of earthly necessity approaches nearer and nearer to it. The exigencies of Northern society may assist traitors to put an end to this war, even if it be not a noble end : the heavy taxes may bring men down on their bellies. The rude state of society in the South — not more complex than an oyster — can co-exist with the rude conditions of war ; but the North will presently find an apology for evading the responsibility it should fulfil ; for it has no right to allow a barbarous Slavery-despotism to build itself upon a half of this continent.

But will foreign powers allow this war to continue indefinitely ?

Revolutions are not bad, sometimes : the revolutions of this planet, for instance : they go on and do not upset the world's universal table, nor rust its loom, nor interfere with France's afternoon cigar. Nay ! by such revolution all these are supplied. It seems to get a slow entrance into the American cerebrum, that in a family of nations, as in a family of individuals, one member is not permitted to throw all the rest into confusion. Enough time is to be allowed for the vindication of national, as of personal individuality ; but when nationality becomes burning down St. Paul's to broil Jonathan's steak, then nationality is the synonyme of nuisance. It is sure to be abated. My American masters, if you desire to have the nations pause

and admire before your Revolution, and not hustle
it off as a sham, let it be one spheral and vital, leading on springtide and waving summer-fields, for you
and for the weary world. Heavens! what an opportunity you have for this!

The most imminent danger now, as it has been from
the first, is that we may be induced by the semi-loyal
States, whose treachery is all the more dangerous because it believes itself the only loyalty, to allow Slavery to remain unburied, to be revived under their
moonshine.

Few as are the slaveholders and the slaves in these
Border States, let us not be deceived into thinking
them of little importance in the issue. There is a
German maxim which reads, " Give the Devil a lock
of your hair, and he will be sure to get your whole
head."

Three Hessian flies only were seen upon the cabin-
wall of a Dutch ship which approached an American
wharf ; now what field in the continent has not known
the devastations of the Hessian fly? Six Norway
rats swam ashore from another Dutch ship in our
waters ; now where is the cellar without them? Two
hundred and forty years ago twenty slaves were brought
to Jamestown, Va., in Dutch ship No. 3 ; — now where
can you go, from Bunker Hill to Sumter, without
hearing the rattle of a slave's chain?

Brothers, let us make a clean sweep of this thing
whilst we are about it!

An ancient Persian scripture says : " Justice is so dear to the heart of Nature, that if at last an atom of injustice should be found, the blue sky would shrivel like a snake-skin to cast it off."

A single slave held in this nation will break it to fragments again, and as often as we try it ; just as a single powder-grain ignited at the heart of the rock of Gibraltar would rive it asunder. Will those who know that the rights of the poorest man are of more importance than a thousand unions, ever keep silent or patient with even *one* fetter in the land ? By God, NEVER !

These slaves of the loyal States we take because they are essential to any permanent peace in the country, and if we are compelled to abnormal strife for peace, we have a military right to strive for a permanent peace, and not merely to defeat an army in this or that engagement. We take these slaves as we have taken the houses and stock of loyal men on our march. Let them bring in their bills. Doubtless we shall have to pay more than the number of loyal slaveholders would warrant ; for we shall be sure to find, when pay-day comes, that every slaveholder had been all along a very Abdiel for fidelity : but who shall stop to count the money that goes to ransom a race and a nation from the slavery which buys and sells the bodies of the one and the souls of the other ?

We shall need liberation *first* in these Border States, not only because we must make a clean sweep of the evil, but because these Border State negroes are to be our guaranties of good faith to the more Southern negroes; they are to be both our banners hung out upon the outer walls, and our telegraph lines along which the electric word of Liberation shall flash.

And here is just where all these confiscation-bills will accomplish nothing real. Every slave would see that Trumbull's bill would end in a transfer of masters, — and he would not respond to it. We must not forget, that between us and those Negroes there stand our mediatorial Marylanders, and darling pets, the Kentuckians, — just sympathetic enough with seceders to buy up claims to and descriptions of running slaves, just star-spangled enough to get back the same from free lines or States, — and from these Border States as from an ark, when the deluge subsided, the South would be repopulated with the same slaves.

Have you, friend, in these late months, sat in the gallery of Congress, heart-sick, hearing everything discussed but the right thing? The hour-hand wheels round and round, and above the clock sits the Muse with motionless pen, the very bronze eye sad that no true movement could she record on her scroll. Confiscation, forfeiture, colonization, — the Southern white man laughs at these, the black man cannot hear them. Does the Negro wish to be exiled? Or does he wish to come North to be kept in jail till two witnesses prove his master a traitor?

My countrymen, you walk a scymitar-bridge to

your Paradise, and the billows of hell underneath receive him who steps one inch, as much as him who
steps a yard, aside.

Sitting there, I was reminded of how an old uncle
of our neighborhood would quiz us. "Boys," he said,
once, "I got a letter from a little boy to-day, and
— ha, ha! — how *do* you think he spelt *dog?*" Then
we all made our guesses, — dogg, doag, dogge, dorg.
At last, when we have exhausted our ingenuity, the
old uncle quietly replies, "Why, he spelt it d-o-g, of
course." Just as idly and as childishly are our rulers
trifling with the sacred hours, to see if something else
cannot be made to wield the divine spell of simple
JUSTICE.

You are praying for and talking of the coming
man. Would he find faith in the land? Are you
quite sure you would not crucify him — or hang him,
as the American way is — should he come? That is
what the Jews did with their Coming Man, after they
had been praying Heaven to send him for four thousand years. Two years ago the wild, half-clad fore-
runner of our coming man, whose meat was wild
honey, was heard in the wilderness of Virginia, and
his head was brought in a charger to Slavery: so
much it cost him to declare the axe laid to the root
of the accursed tree. How little does this nation
know what a right and true man, should he break
into our midst, would do with us! Little see we the
piled shreds of broken red-tape, — little the moun-

tain of the refuse of epaulets and brass buttons!
He would re-distribute Washington into the original
elements, and gather it for loam about the roots of
the sapling he would rear.

Yet pray on, O people, for the coming man! Not
as you expect it shall be his advent; but he shall
come, and before the masses are ready for him.
Somewhere the granite is crystallizing for his bones;
somewhere the metal is refining for his blood; somewhere Nature is fashioning the exquisite lobes of his
brain: presently America's maternal cry shall be
heard, and THE MAN shall clasp hands with THE
HOUR.

When it is understood to be absolutely certain that
the honest masses of this country are determined
never again to compromise with Slavery, nor to allow it the protection of this government, then the
national saviour will come, by whose life and death
the nation will be saved. But do these honest masses
realize that, if a compromise, involving an amnesty
to Slavery, should be proposed by the Confederates to
our Cabinet and Congress as at present organized, it
would certainly be accepted?

Up, hearts of America, and let your irrevocable
"GET THEE BEHIND US!" thunder at the gates of the
capital, and go crashing through the South, a bomb
whose flame cannot be extinguished! Let Slavery
know that it shall never, never find peace in this nation; let your rulers know that, if they shall give you

a Union with Slavery in it, you will make of it such a Union as fire and gunpowder make!

The men who are to save this nation, if it is to be saved, are those who see that it must and should rise or fall with simple justice; and those who strive for a Free Republic must see eye to eye.

There is not one fibre of moral earnestness, not one atom of fidelity or conviction, more than is needed to rescue the nation from terrible dissolution, or the worse fate of a Union sealed in its dishonor. All hearts must work, and they must work together.

The best friend of freedom in the government is the President. But in this matter he has refused to lead. Repeatedly he said, "If the people feel so, let them organize their will and pass it through Congress," — ignoring the fact that the people had set him apart from their millions to organize from the *feeling* of the masses an operative will. Then, coming up among the people, they all said, "We had best leave all this to the President: he is at the centre, and knows more than we do; he'll do the right thing at the right time." And so the President and the people have been all along playing at battle-door with the Slavery question, each tossing it to the other to be dealt with. At length Old Abe agrees to take a step. Borrowing a good idea from his former occupation, he inserts the smallest edge of a wedge into a small crack of the log; then he says to Congress and the people, " Now, if you want to split that

log, the way is to strike that wedge." Let us take
the President at his word, and strike!

How can you strike? Let every man, woman, and
child in this nation send his or her prayer to the
Capitol to have Slavery abolished. And warn your
representative to help this measure or hang himself
on Capitol Hill before coming back. You need not
be particular about the way: where there's a will,
there's a way. All these technicalities are so much
thin disguise for a wavering purpose: let Congress or
the President rise to the point of striking Slavery
dead, and whether they are States or Territories, or
whether Andy Johnson is a military or civic officer,
will be but a strife of words.

The right to open schools for Negroes in North
Carolina, against the laws of that State, includes the
right to set every slave in it free.

Upon the North the guilt of this Rebellion is
heaviest; and upon the North the retribution will be
heaviest. The North has been cruel to the South, —
cruel as is he who continues to trust to an infant the
knife with which it has already gashed its flesh.

O Northern Conscience, trace honestly the blood-
drippings of this Rebellion, even if they lead to thine
own door!

If one should see a fellow-man drinking poison, and
should not strain every sinew to stop it, the law holds
him justly as the suicide's murderer. How long have
you sat with folded arms seeing your Southern brother

drinking this vile drug, which has finally maddened him! How long did your representatives, your clergy-men, your merchants, cry *Hush* to all who lifted up the warning voice, — whilst to the slave's cry your ears were stopped with cotton, to his oppressor your tongue was sweetened with sugar? And now when, having gone forward upon the logical path, cleared by your-selves, — mobbing and hanging all who would have saved them, — they reach the inevitable climax of their fearful disease, still you will not be humane enough to take the poison from their lips; even now you are talking in cold blood about Jamaica and sugar, and whether by emancipation sugar rose a cent or a cent and a quarter; still, whilst your left eye is on your banner, your right is on your hogshead!

Nearly every human being sharing the blood of him who writes these words is arrayed against this country. You think them guilty traitors? But I remember how Northern preachers proved to them that they stood upon the Rock of Ages, how to them Northern repre-sentatives cried, " Great is Slavery, and the Constitution is its prophet! " — and I will not fling hard names at them, lest they should strike leading Union men who deserted the South at the one moment when there might have been some courage in clinging to her; the

"Ever strong upon the stronger side."

But you, true-hearted Northmen, I implore, ere you go further in this butchery, to try if you cannot SAVE the South. What if this Republic should be gasping for a simple breath of justice, — the very atmosphere of Liberty! At least shall we not wash our hands of their guilt concerning the crushed black and the equally crushed white of the South? O, is there no power in Love greater than any that Hate can wield? Is there no strength in Eternal Justice? Is there in this noon of the nineteenth century so little power of heart and brain that we must yet adhere to the methods of the savage and the assassin?

We smile to-day at the heathen of antiquity who hesitated whether he would make his log into a god or a three-legged stool; but our children may weep in the retrospect of this day, when a great nation, with its government before it to be necessarily refashioned, hesitated whether to make of it a centralization whose three legs must be Southern barbarism, Northern demoralization, and perpetual strife, or a godlike Union impregnable as Justice itself.

Courage, brothers! much as the Devil has to do with it, this world still belongs to God.

Be not entangled in the illusions which twine about and bind your rulers. Slavery seems to them a strong thing; so mariners have mistaken a fog-bank for the rock of Gibraltar. There is not a mushroom that grows which is not stronger than Slavery, against which every whispering wind, every sunbeam, every leaf, and every human blood-drop is conspiring. I know that our government sees it as a strong steed without which it cannot ride to victory in the South ; but it is a stick horse which it childishly carries, maintaining that it is carried by it : just let the government stop carrying Slavery, and it will fall the dead stick that it is. I challenge the President to permit me — one of the weakest and obscurest friends of Freedom — to liberate the slaves of the South, *promising only that I shall not be interfered with by United States law.* I will not call for any protection by its arms from the Southerners ; the law of gravitation will bear the small stone cut from the mountain-top down its sides, even to the gulf.

The whining and cursing of the pro-slavery men in Congress are a confession that Slavery, with its swashing and martial outside, is conscious of this essential weakness. Those Border State men know well that the winds and rains and heats of this thawing season have made its crust so thin that it will not bear the pressure of one firm foot. And, alas ! the indecent eagerness with which the President hastened to refasten the gyves upon a million human beings whom the noble Hunter had set free, — AND WHO ARE FREE, — engenders the saddest misgiving of the hour ; namely, that the President knows the weakness of Slavery, knows that he could free the land forever from that crime and its retribution now heavy upon us, but heeds some baser end to be subserved by retaining this institution.

A million blood-stains crimson your hands, Mr. President; damned spots, which not all the rivers and lakes in America can wash away; but in one globule of ink upon your table you may wash them away. If *your* Golden Hour shall pass, and those beings you have cruelly robbed remain slaves, the time will come when you will pray bitterly to be able to exchange your lot with the lowliest, most deeply wronged slave in South Carolina!

But even with all these powers enlisted to sustain that institution (!), which without them could not stand one day, it is not, brothers, a formidable foe, if we can bring to confront it the true and spotless spirit of Liberty.

Strong as the other is weak — chief among those perilous rudimentary laws which, being bred in the bone of the world, must come out in the flesh — is Liberty. There is a story of a chemist who undertook with powerful agents to extract a birth-mark from his wife's cheek. After a long while he drew it out, but he drew her life with it. Liberty is the birth-mark of man, as it is his birthright; and when man ceases to love Liberty, it will be because his race has become extinct.

The spirit of Liberty is as ancient as the most conservative could desire; it began with the first throb of life which ever stirred the heart of Nature. From that heart comes the ascending scale of life, each higher animal form differing from that which preceded it simply by its greater freedom. Where the oyster was anchored to a rock, the fish moves freely; where the blossom was bound to the stem, the butterfly comes, a freed blossom. Each form was only a revolutionary effort for more independent life. The human form, when it appeared, was the last and the decisive battle of the animal to rise up from the earth, and stand free and erect, by that sign sovereign of the planet. Thus the everlasting burden of Nature rolls through the echoing caverns of past epochs, and bursts up in the hearts and tongues sent from her womb to cry aloud, and to struggle endlessly for Liberty. When man first wronged his brother, that brother's blood cried to heaven from this same old earth; and, until the last wrong is righted and the last of her children free, her mother's heart will heave with pain, and utter its uncontrollable protest, to be followed, if unheeded, with fiercer earthquakes than these.

Admit not, then, into your hearts a single fear for Liberty's cause with her impotent antagonist, whatever fears you may have that this proud government, having deliberately taken the side of Slavery, may be buried in its grave, which every bayonet, North and South, is digging, and equally. But not to that end, nor for that reason, should a true and faithful heart seize the bayonet or other implement, whether the government call or command. Rather let each friend of his country plant himself upon his loyalty to that which is higher than the banner of the Union,—

the banner of Liberty; with that sacred ensign float-ing over him, let him stand or be stricken down. Up, hearts, and let each deliver his own soul! Up, and the government will be forced to obey you, for you will bear the tables of eternal law in your hands! Men need not be dozing in a White House, or wran-gling in a Capitol, to be strong: each step upward in office marks another shackle assumed. But true hearts are free, — free to stand, or be hanged, if need be, — and Liberty may yet need her martyrs in the North.

If this country is to be saved, the Abolitionists are to save it; and, though they seem few in numbers, they are not by a thousandth so few as were Chris-tians when Jesus suffered, or Protestants when Luther spoke. There is need only that we should stand as one man, and unto the end, for an absolutely Free Republic, swearing to promote eternal strife until it be attained, — until in waters which Agitation, the angel of Freedom, has troubled, the diseased nation shall bathe, and be made every whit whole.

The Golden Hour is before us: there is in America enough wisdom and courage to coin it, ere it passes, into national honor and peace, if it is all put forth.

Up, hearts!

THE END.

Cambridge : Stereotyped and Printed by Welch, Bigelow, & Co.